Mathematical Aspects of
Numerical Grid Generation

Frontiers in Applied Mathematics

Frontiers in Applied Mathematics is a series that presents new mathematical or computational approaches to significant scientific problems. Beginning with Volume 4, the series reflects a change in both philosophy and format. Each volume focuses on a broad application of general interest to applied mathematicians as well as engineers and other scientists.

This unique series will advance the development of applied mathematics through the rapid publication of short, inexpensive books that lie on the cutting edge of research.

Frontiers in Applied Mathematics

Mathematical Aspects of Numerical Grid Generation

Edited by José E. Castillo
San Diego State University

Society for Industrial and Applied Mathematics
siam.
Philadelphia 1991

Library of Congress Cataloging-in-Publication Data

Mathematical aspects of numerical grid generation / edited by José E.
    Castillo.
            p. cm. -- (Frontiers in applied mathematics : 8)
        Includes bibliographical references and index.
        ISBN 0-89871-267-X
        1. Numerical grid generation (Numerical analysis) I. Castillo,
    José E. II. Series
    QA377.M284 1991
    515'.353--dc20   91-14973
                                                                                  CIP

To Fania, Claudia, and Igor

Contents

Contributors

José E. Castillo, Department of Mathematical Sciences, San Diego State University, San Diego, California 92182

Arkady Dvinsky, Creare Inc., P.O. Box 71, Etna Road, Hanover, New Hampshire 03755

Patrick M. Knupp, Ecodynamics Research Associates Inc., P.O. Box 8172, Albuquerque, New Mexico 87198

Gordon Liao, Department of Mathematics, University of Texas, Arlington, Texas 76019

C. Wayne Mastin, Department of Mathematics, Drawer A, Mississippi State University, Mississippi State, Mississippi 39762

Patrick J. Roache, Ecodynamics Research Associates Inc., P. O. Box 8172, Albuquerque, New Mexico 87198

S. S. Sritharan, Department of Aerospace Engineering, University of Southern California, Los Angeles, California 90089

Stanly Steinberg, Department of Mathematics and Statistics, University of New Mexico, Albuquerque, New Mexico 87131

Z. U. A. Warsi, Department of Aerospace Engineering, Drawer A, Mississippi State University, Mississippi State, Mississippi 39762

Foreword

The present SIAM publication on the mathematical aspects of grid generation is a welcome addition to the literature on boundary-fitted grid generation, a subject of first-rank importance to computational physics and engineering.

The literature of boundary-fitted grid generation has suffered because the subject is too easy. There are many methods which produce, at least, a marginally acceptable grid for a particular geometry. Consequently, there exists an abundance of ad hoc techniques, but a scarcity of analysis, real understanding, and generality. The "experiences" of engineering practitioners (like myself) are often misleading, since individual researchers often work within a narrow class of problems. We have seen in the literature supposedly robust methods which, when applied to new problems, either failed to converge or resulted in folded grids—methods which, for a mild range of boundary parameters, produced results which were not unique, i.e., for which the final grid depended on the initial grid condition, and methods which produce unacceptable skewing. Likewise, solution adaptivity functions offer ample opportunity for *creative* but arbitrary inventiveness; virtually anything "works," but there is little rational basis for selecting one method over another.

It should be obvious that not all aspects of grid generation could be covered in this publication. Noticeably absent are algebraic methods, unstructured grids, substructured grids, triangular grids, and polygonal grids. There is not much emphasis on solution adaptivity and what is found herein is r-type adaptivity, i.e., redistribution of a fixed number of gridpoints, rather than h-type adaptivity (in which the number of gridpoints is increased) or p-type adaptivity (in which the support of elements is enriched).

Dr. Castillo is to be congratulated for organizing the SIAM minisymposia, and he and Dr. Steinberg are to be congratulated for organizing this publication. It is hoped that future SIAM meetings will also contribute to the late-blooming mathematical analysis of grid-generation algorithms.

Patrick J. Roache
April 1990

Preface

Numerical grid generation plays a critical role in any scientific computing problem when the geometry of the underlying region is complex or when the solution has a complex structure. For example, to model the air flow about an airplane, points must be chosen outside the airplane. Even for simple models, the number of points needed is in the millions. In the most elementary models, the points should be uniformly distributed. For more general models, the gridpoints near the boundary may need to be many orders of magnitude more dense than the points far from the boundary. In the situation where there are shock waves in the flow, points near the shock need to be many orders of magnitude more dense than the points far from the shock. However, note that typically there is no a priori way to determine the position of the shock. When the gridpoints are chosen so that some of the points "line up" with the boundary, then the grid is boundary conforming, boundary adapted, or geometry adapted. When the gridpoints depend on some feature of the solution of the problem, then the solution is solution-adapted.

Even with current software tools, the generation of a grid in a scientific computing problem accounts for a substantial portion of the effort needed to solve the problem. Thus, the goal of much grid-generation research is the creation of robust and automatic grid-generation algorithms. "Automatic" means that the amount of human effort needed to generate the grid is reduced by using more computing resources. "Robust" means that the grid-generation algorithm produces suitable grids over a wide range of regions and that the grids are not sensitive to small changes in the region. One means to guarantee that the algorithm is robust is to prove that it generates a unique solution that depends "continuously" on the region and that the solution corresponds to a "reasonable" grid. Unfortunately, no one has yet rigorously defined a concept of "reasonable" that applies to a wide range of grids.

Many grid-generation algorithms have a continuum limit; that is, as the distance between gridpoints goes to zero, the limiting grid distribution becomes a transformation that is a solution to a boundary value problem for a partial differential equation or variational equation. In this situation, the notion of "reasonable" can be defined by requiring the transformation to be one-to-one and onto. The notion of "robust" becomes the notion of a well-posed problem for the boundary value problem. The fact that the continuum problem is well posed does not imply that the grid-generation algorithm is robust. However, this well-posedness indicates that the discrete problem should be well posed for sufficiently high resolution.

Very little mathematical work has been done on grid-generation problems. The purpose of this volume is to begin a discussion of the mathematical aspects of grid generation that will provide a deeper understanding of the algorithms and their limitations. The work presented in this volume is based on the papers presented at the two minisymposia, "Numerical Grid Generation: Mathematical Aspects, Parts I and II," held at the SIAM Annual Meeting in Minneapolis, Minnesota, in July 1988.

Acknowledgment

Part of this work was done while the editor was visiting the Department of Mathematics at the University of New Mexico. The editor thanks the department for its assistance and, particularly, Linda Cicarella for her expert help with LaTeX. The editor also thanks Holly Wilson for proofreading parts of the manuscript. My deepest gratitude goes to Professor Steinberg for making the completion of this volume possible.

José E. Castillo
San Diego

Chapter 1

Introduction

J. E. Castillo and S. Steinberg

When a continuum modeling problem is solved numerically, it is necessary to convert the continuum to a finite set of points. The choice of points is determined by grid generation. In simple problems, the grid can be chosen a priori. If the geometry of the problems is simple but the solution of the problem has a complicated structure, as is the case for many initial-value problems for ordinary differential equations, then the grid should be adapted to the features of the solution. Solution algorithms that automatically choose the stepsize or order of the method are solution adaptive. If the problem involves a nontrivial region in two- or three-dimensional space, then the discrete set of points in the region should be adapted to the shape of the region. Choosing such a set of points gives a boundary-fitted (boundary-conforming, boundary-adapted, geometry-adapted) grid. In addition, if the solution of the modeling problem has a complicated structure, then the grid should be adapted to these features, becoming both a solution- and geometry-adapted grid.

Once a grid is chosen, the equations describing the model must be discretized and solved. Models that are described by initial-value and boundary-value problems for partial differential equations (PDEs) are frequently encountered, although integral equations and variational problems are also common. The discretization can be done using finite-difference, finite-element, finite-volume, and other techniques. Many grid-generation techniques and their applications to a wide variety of problems can be found in the proceedings [22], [32], [33], [37], [60], [73].

There are two distinct approaches to discretizing a region: structured and unstructured. This book considers only structured grids; for information on unstructured grids, see [60]. A structured grid can be viewed as a mapping from an index space to a physical space. If the index space is identified with a lattice of points in a rectangular region (called "logical space"), then the continuum limit of the grid gives a mapping of logical space to physical space as the number of points increases. Since the continuum map must be invertible, it can also be thought of as a map from physical to logical space. Many of the results in this book are for continuum maps. If the continuum map is well

1

behaved, it is hoped that this will imply that the discrete map will inherit this good behavior. As will be shown, this hope has not been well-realized for many algorithms.

Some years ago, there was discovered an intimate connection between some of the partial differential equations, variational algorithms, and the differential-geometric notion of a harmonic map. Note that the word "harmonic" is used in two different but related ways in this book: (1) there is the classical notion of a harmonic function as the solution of the homogeneous Laplace equation, and (2) the notion of a harmonic map as a transformation of R^n to R^n for which each component is harmonic. The notion of a harmonic map can be extended to mappings of manifolds of equal dimension; the components of such maps satisfy a Laplace–Beltrami equation. In addition, the notion of a harmonic map has a variational formulation in which the map minimizes an energy functional.

Grid generation is a relatively new discipline; some early papers that influenced the field are: Winslow [85]; Amsden and Hirt [2]; Thompson, Thames, and Mastin [74]; Eiseman [87]; and Brackbill and Saltzman [11]. Reviews of the field are given in Thompson [71] and Eiseman [29]. Grid-generation methods can be conveniently grouped as follows: hand and elementary methods; interpolation, or algebraic methods; partial differential equation methods; and variational methods. An overview of these methods can be obtained from Thompson, Warsi, and Mastin [75]. Together, these techniques provide powerful tools for solving many important problems. However, many practitioners report substantial difficulties with existing algorithms when they start new problems. The grids produced will be badly skewed, compressed, expanded, or even folded in some parts of the region, or the grid-generation algorithm will not converge at all. To produce more robust algorithms, it is imperative that one have a deeper mathematical understanding of the limitations and strengths of the existing algorithms. This volume is a step in that direction.

The main emphasis of this book is on gaining a mathematical understanding of grid-generation algorithms, with particular attention being paid to variational, or PDE methods. However, there is still much to be learned about algebraic methods, as is shown in Chapter 6. Moreover, much can be learned about modern methods by looking back to classical harmonic functions and conformal mappings, as is done in Chapter 2. In Chapter 7, classical differential geometry is used to produce grid-generation algorithms. The connection between harmonic maps and grid-generation algorithms in two dimensions is explored in several chapters. In Chapter 8, harmonic maps are used to create practical grid-generation algorithms. Some basic results (both positive and negative) for harmonic maps are proved in Chapters 9 and 10. The implications of these results for grid-generation algorithms is discussed in Chapters 8, 9, and 10. There are still important open questions about harmonic maps in three dimensions.

All of the PDE methods have an equivalent variational formulation in which the differential equations are the Euler–Lagrange equations of a minimization problem (see Chapters 3, 9, and 10). On the other hand, variational formulations can be directly derived from elementary geometric consideration. This produces three types of functionals: one for controlling grid spacing or smoothness, in which the minimizers are harmonic maps; one for controlling the area or volume of grid cells; and a third one for controlling the angles between grid lines. In Chapter 3, the existence and uniqueness of solutions to the continuum variational problem are treated for the smoothness problem. Some of these results are extended to the area functional.

Most of the analytic grid-generation methods emphasize discretizing the Euler–Lagrange equations. However, it is also reasonable to discretize the functional directly and then solve the resulting discrete minimization problem. In fact, this approach has a serious pitfall [16]. In Chapter 4, it is shown that the pitfall can be avoided by directly deriving a functional from the discrete geometry and then minimizing that functional. This produces a robust and efficient algorithm for controlling multiple grid properties.

In addition to the open questions in the continuum, there are significant differences between the discrete and continuum theories. In Chapter 5, it is shown that the bifurcation diagrams for an elementary problem are drastically different in the continuum and discrete cases. Additional problems of this type are also identified in Chapters 2, 4, and 8.

The following list contains a brief description of each chapter:

In Chapter 2, Mastin considers the connection between classical conformal mappings and elliptic and variational grid generation. Grid folding can be avoided by examining the underlying mathematical connections between these methods.

In Chapter 3, Castillo discusses the existence and uniqueness of solutions to the continuum variational grid-generation problems for both smoothness and area control. Classification of the Euler–Lagrange equations is presented, and the replication of a reference grid is analyzed.

In Chapter 4, Castillo discusses a discrete variational formulation based directly on the geometry of the discrete grid. The grid produced by the discrete length control functional is shown to converge to the optimal grid produced by the smoothness functional used by Steinberg and Roache. Also, a model problem is used to show that the discrete area functional has bifurcations.

In Chapter 5, Steinberg and Roache show that the variational curve grid-generation algorithms, which involve the solution of discrete nonlinear algebraic equations, have bifurcation properties significantly different from their continuum limits.

In Chapter 6, Knupp introduces and analyzes three alternatives to the transfinite interpolation algorithm. "Transfinite interpolation" is an algebraic grid-generation algorithm that maps the full boundary of logical space to the boundary of physical space. Methods with this property are transcendental, i.e., not polynomial. The new algorithms are called *intrinsic* algebraic grid-generation methods because they do not require blending functions. On the other hand, the new algorithms are sensitive to the placement of the physical region. Substantial insight into the transfinite and intrinsic algorithms is gained by studying their behavior under elementary transformations of physical space.

In Chapter 7, Warsi obtains surface grid-generation algorithms from the Gauss and Weingarten equations of classical differential geometry.

In Chapter 8, Dvinsky uses differential-geometric harmonic maps to produce useful grid-generation algorithms. The theory of harmonic maps (see also Chapters 9 and 10) provides a strong mathematical basis for the algorithms. Inverses of harmonic maps are typically not harmonic; consequently, there are two possible types of harmonic maps. This is illuminated in two dimensions, where the classical elliptic methods are shown to be special cases of the differential geometric approach. As with other methods, if the nonlinear terms in the Laplace–Beltrami equations are large, elementary numerical approaches have problems that can be corrected by improving the discretization of the PDEs. Solution adaptivity can be included in the Riemannian metric. This idea is applied to a two-dimensional convection-diffusion equation.

In Chapter 9, Liao introduces harmonic maps as minima of an energy functional and shows that such maps satisfy the Laplace–Beltrami equations. It is shown that in the two-dimensional planar case, a classical theorem of Rado implies that the harmonic map is a homeomorphism. The main point of this chapter is to analyze the three-dimensional Euclidean case to understand why it is so difficult. To this end, a proof of Rado's theorem is given and then an example provided by Lewy is used to show that the generalization to three dimensions is much more involved. The distinctions between two and three dimensions can be further illuminated by studying the singularities of harmonic maps. Again, the one-to-one nature of three-dimensional maps is left as an open question.

In Chapter 10, Sritharan, using the theory of Sobolev spaces, shows that the differential geometric notion of a harmonic map has an equivalent variational formulation and the solutions of the variational problem have a regularity property. In two dimensions these results are extended to show that there is a unique harmonic map of general regions to convex regions that is a homeomorphism. This result can be extended to three dimensions, except for the map being one-to-one, which is left as an open problem.

This book by no means answers all the mathematical questions arising in grid generation; however, it presents some of the most important aspects of mathematics of grid generation being considered by the contributors at this time.

1.1. Notation

Given a region in two dimensions, the mathematical planar grid-generation problem is to construct a transformation between this region and another region that will be used as a computational space. The given region is called *physical space*, while the computational region is called *logical space*. If physical space is described using the variables x and y, while logical space is described using the variables ξ and η, then the continuum transformation can be written as

(1.1)
$$x = x(\xi, \eta), \qquad y = y(\xi, \eta)$$

(see Fig. 1.1). It is assumed that the transformation maps the square *one-*

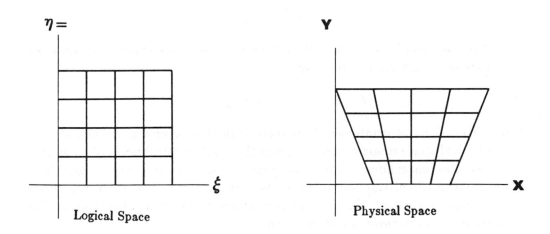

FIG. 1.1. *Logical and physical space.*

to-one and *onto* the physical region, that the boundary is included, and that boundaries are preserved. There are a number of names associated with such transformations: *boundary conforming, boundary adapted, boundary fitted*. In the boundary-conforming case, the boundaries of the physical region are given by the following four curves:

$$(x(\xi,0), y(\xi,0)), \qquad 0 \le \xi \le 1,$$
$$(x(\xi,1), y(\xi,1)), \qquad 0 \le \xi \le 1,$$
$$(x(0,\eta), y(0,\eta)), \qquad 0 \le \eta \le 1,$$
$$(x(1,\eta), y(1,\eta)), \qquad 0 \le \eta \le 1.$$

It is typical to assume that the transformation is at least *continuously differentiable*. Then the one-to-one property can be guaranteed by requiring that the *Jacobian* of the transformation not be zero in the region. Actually, it is important to assume that the Jacobian is uniformly bounded below and above in the closed unit square, i.e., the Jacobian is well behaved near the boundary of the region. If partial derivatives are abbreviated using subscripts,

$$(1.2) \qquad x_\xi = \frac{\partial x}{\partial \xi}, \qquad x_\eta = \frac{\partial x}{\partial \eta}, \qquad y_\xi = \frac{\partial y}{\partial \xi}, \qquad y_\eta = \frac{\partial y}{\partial \eta},$$

then the *Jacobian matrix* is given by

$$(1.3) \qquad M = \begin{bmatrix} x_\xi & x_\eta \\ y_\xi & y_\eta \end{bmatrix},$$

and the Jacobian is given by the determinant of the Jacobian matrix:

$$(1.4) \qquad J = x_\xi\, y_\eta - x_\eta\, y_\xi\,.$$

If the Jacobian is never zero, then the inverse-function theorem guarantees the existence of a local inverse map

$$(1.5) \qquad \xi = \xi(x,y)\,, \qquad \eta = \eta(x,y)\,.$$

Some discussions of grid generation start with this inverse map, i.e., a map from physical space to logical space. From the mathematical point of view, this makes no difference; however, the reader interested in implementing algorithms needs to keep the distinction between these maps clear. The chain rule gives the following formulas, which relate derivatives of the transformation to the derivatives of the inverse transformation:

$$(1.6) \quad x_\xi = \eta_y/J\,, \qquad x_\eta = -\xi_y/J\,, \qquad y_\xi = -\eta_x/J\,, \qquad y_\eta = \xi_x/J\,.$$

To compare these formulas to those of others, one must take care to understand whether or not the formulas use the Jacobian of the transformation J or the Jacobian of the inverse transformation $\tilde{J}$. Recall that the chain rule also gives $J\tilde{J} = 1$.

The transformation can be thought of as inducing general curvilinear coordinates in physical space. If a and b are constants with $0 \le a, b \le 1$, then the coordinate lines are given by the two families of curves

$$\begin{aligned}
(x(a,\eta),\, y(a,\eta))\,, \quad 0 \le \eta \le 1\,, \\
(x(\xi,b),\, y(\xi,b))\,, \quad 0 \le \xi \le 1\,.
\end{aligned}$$

In general, these two families of curves are not orthogonal, i.e., the curvilinear coordinates are not orthogonal coordinates.

In three dimensions most of the above notation is changed in a straightforward way. Thus physical space is described using the variables x, y, and z, whereas logical space is described using the variables ξ, η, and ζ. The formula for the Jacobian is

$$(1.7) \quad J = +x_\xi y_\eta z_\zeta + x_\eta y_\zeta z_\xi + x_\zeta y_\xi z_\eta - x_\xi y_\zeta z_\eta - x_\eta y_\xi z_\zeta - x_\zeta y_\eta z_\xi .$$

The formulas for transforming derivatives of the transformation become more complicated:

$$
\begin{aligned}
&x_\xi = \frac{\eta_y \zeta_z - \zeta_y \eta_z}{J} ; &\quad &y_\xi = \frac{\zeta_x \eta_z - \eta_x \zeta_z}{J} ; &\quad &z_\xi = \frac{\eta_x \zeta_y - \zeta_x \eta_y}{J} ; \\
(1.8) \quad &x_\eta = \frac{\zeta_y \xi_z - \xi_y \zeta_z}{J} ; &\quad &y_\eta = \frac{\xi_x \zeta_z - \zeta_x \xi_z}{J} ; &\quad &z_\eta = \frac{\zeta_x \xi_y - \xi_x \zeta_y}{J} ; \\
&x_\zeta = \frac{\xi_y \eta_z - \eta_y \xi_z}{J} ; &\quad &y_\zeta = \frac{\eta_x \xi_z - \xi_x \eta_z}{J} ; &\quad &z_\zeta = \frac{\xi_x \eta_y - \eta_x \xi_y}{J} .
\end{aligned}
$$

In some mathematical discussions, the distinction between physical and logical space does not play a role. Thus one can look at transformations between two regions or, more generally, between two differentiable manifolds. The fundamental question for grid generation is: Given two regions of the same dimension, is there a one-to-one and onto transformation between the regions? More importantly, if such a transformation exists, can a practical construction be provided for it?

Chapter 2

Elliptic Grid Generation and Conformal Mapping

C. W. Mastin

2.1. Introduction

The theoretical foundations of elliptic grid generation owe much to the theory of conformal mappings, which preceded it by several decades. In fact, the main impetus for the development of elliptic methods was the lack of versatility in the construction of conformal maps and the inability to control the distribution of gridpoints in the generated grid. It is interesting to note that the successful elliptic methods were those that were borrowed most heavily from the properties of conformal mappings. The objective of this report is to examine elliptic methods of grid generation and to see how they are related to conformal mappings. In some cases where undesirable properties such as grid folding occur, the problem can be avoided by going back and reexamining the theoretical development of the method.

While conformal mappings are practical only in two dimensions, some of the fundamental mapping properties can be carried over to the construction of three-dimensional grids. Here again, the information can be used to explain why certain grid-generating equations fail while others generate usable three-dimensional grids.

Most of the grid-generation methods discussed are well known, and their ability to generate useful grids is understood. Therefore, only a few examples of computational grids will be given. The main objective is to show how problems encountered in grid generation can be solved by returning to the foundations of conformal mapping.

2.2. Two-Dimensional Grid Generation

In two dimensions there is a close relationship between elliptic grid-generation methods and conformal mappings. This can be seen by considering the conformal mapping of a simply connected region D in the xy-plane onto a rectangular region R in the $\xi\eta$-plane. The conformal mapping determines the aspect ratio of the rectangular region. Thus if the width of the rectangle is set to unity, its height must be some conformal invariant quantity M, which is referred to as the module of the region D. Now the mapping of D onto R and its inverse satisfy the Cauchy–Riemann equations, which can be written as

$$\xi_x = \eta_y,$$
$$\xi_y = -\eta_x$$

or

$$x_\xi = y_\eta,$$
$$x_\eta = -y_\xi.$$

Based on these equations, it is noted that both ξ and η (as functions of x and y) and x and y (as functions of ξ and η) satisfy Laplace's equation. Now any simply connected region can be mapped onto a square region S if an additional stretching transformation is used. Thus, consider the following change of variables:

$$\nu = \frac{\eta}{M},$$
$$\mu = \xi.$$

The composite mapping is not conformal and the mapping functions satisfy the following first-order systems, which now include the module of R as a parameter:

$$\mu_x = M\nu_y,$$
$$\mu_y = -M\nu_x$$

or

(2.1)
$$M x_\mu = y_\nu,$$
$$x_\nu = -M y_\mu.$$

For this mapping onto a square region, μ and ν are harmonic functions so that

(2.2)
$$\mu_{xx} + \mu_{yy} = 0,$$
$$\nu_{xx} + \nu_{yy} = 0,$$

but x and y satisfy the system

(2.3)
$$M^2 x_{\mu\mu} + x_{\nu\nu} = 0,$$
$$M^2 y_{\mu\mu} + y_{\nu\nu} = 0.$$

The following relation can also be derived from the above first-order system (2.1):

$$M^2 = \frac{x_\nu^2 + y_\nu^2}{x_\mu^2 + y_\mu^2}.$$

In the field of grid generation, it is the harmonic mapping from the region D to the square S that has been most important. It was noted that even with Dirichlet boundary conditions, the mapping is one-to-one and a nonfolding grid can be constructed by inverting the system and solving the resulting nonlinear system on the square. It can easily be shown that the mapping defined as the solution of (2.2), with boundary conditions given by a one-to-one correspondence between the boundary of D and the boundary of S, satisfies the following properties:

1. All points of D map into S; i.e., there is no grid folding or spillover.
2. The gradients $\nabla\mu$ and $\nabla\nu$ do not vanish on D.
3. The Jacobian $J = \mu_x\nu_y - \mu_y\nu_x$ is nonvanishing in D.

These results are well known and have been generalized in recent papers by Smith and Sritharan [63] and Dvinsky [24]. Only a few comments on the proofs of these properties will be made. Property 1 is a result of the maximum and minimum principles for harmonic functions. Property 2 follows by applying the argument principle to the analytic function having μ (or ν) as its real part and noting that a vanishing derivative would contradict the assumed boundary correspondence. Using the results of properties 1 and 2, property 3 can be verified by noting that $J/ \parallel \nabla\mu \parallel^2$ is a harmonic function and, assuming the orientation of the boundary contour is preserved under the mapping, is nonnegative on the boundary of D. Thus the Jacobian would be positive by the maximum principle. The details of the proof of property 2 may be found in the paper by Mastin and Thompson [48]. The proof of property 3 is motivated by comments in the paper of Godunov and Prokopov [35]. An alternate proof given in [48] contains an error.

The one disadvantage of constructing the harmonic mapping of D onto S is that the inverse does satisfy a nonlinear system. However, the system, which is given below, is quasilinear and can usually be solved by almost any method for solving general elliptic equations:

(2.4)
$$\alpha x_{\mu\mu} - 2\beta x_{\mu\nu} + \gamma x_{\nu\nu} = 0,$$
$$\alpha y_{\mu\mu} - 2\beta y_{\mu\nu} + \gamma y_{\nu\nu} = 0,$$

where

$$\alpha = x_\nu^2 + y_\nu^2,$$
$$\beta = x_\mu x_\nu + y_\mu y_\nu,$$
$$\gamma = x_\mu^2 + y_\mu^2.$$

Since the above mapping requires the solution of a nonlinear system of equations, there has been a continuing interest in attempting to generate grids by solving system (2.3) with Dirichlet boundary conditions. The main difficulty is the need for a reasonably good estimate of M. This problem was first addressed by Barfield [6], who noted that grid folding could occur with the wrong value of M. This fact has been rediscovered many times by researchers attempting to generate grids on nonconvex regions D by constructing a harmonic mapping of S onto D. Although no easily computable and accurate estimate of M is known, the value used by Barfield has worked well in numerous cases. That value may be expressed as the integral

$$M = \int\int_S \left[\frac{x_\nu^2 + y_\nu^2}{x_\mu^2 + y_\mu^2} \right]^{1/2} d\mu \, d\nu.$$

Note that if system (2.1) is satisfied, the integral would be the constant M. In practice, iterative methods are used to solve the equations of grid generation, and this integral represents the average aspect ratio of some initial grid.

The following examples give typical grids constructed by the methods mentioned above. The same boundary correspondence was used in all three cases. Figure 2.1 is a grid constructed by system (2.4). Figure 2.2 contains a grid constructed by system (2.3), with a value of $M = 1$, which is not close to the correct value for this region. Note that the grid folds and the mapping is not one-to-one or onto. The grid in Fig. 2.3 was also constructed using (2.3), but the value of M was computed from a grid constructed by interpolation from the boundary values of the mapping. No folding of the grid occurs, but there are points where the Jacobian is very small. While grid folding with $M = 1$ occurs only for nonconvex regions, even for convex regions the skewness of the grid can often be decreased by using a better value of M. In cases where the desired grid would have different aspect ratios in different parts of the region, a variable value for M has also worked well. The problem of grid folding has been treated in several ways. A different approach to the problem has been proposed by Castillo, Steinberg, and Roache [18].

Since the theory of conformal mappings of rectangular regions onto surfaces parallels the results for mappings onto plane regions, the same conclusions can be drawn. The elliptic equations for mapping a region on a surface in three-dimensional space should be derived by considering the equations satisfied by an appropriately scaled conformal mapping. For a conformal mapping, the parametric variables of the surface satisfy a first-order system of partial differential equations called the Beltrami equations. The mapping between the rectangular region and the parametric space of the surface is a quasi-conformal mapping. When the mapping is scaled, the parametric variables s and t satisfy a system of the following form:

$$M s_\mu = a t_\nu - b s_\nu,$$
$$M t_\mu = b t_\nu - c s_\nu.$$

The coefficients a, b, and c derive from the parametric equations defining the surface. Thus we see again that the second-order linear system satisfied by s and t does include the parameter M, which represents the aspect ratio of the cells in surface grid. Alternately, a second-order system can be derived

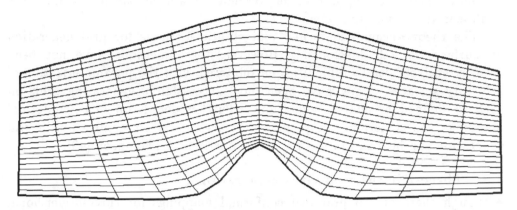

FIG. 2.1. *Grid from the harmonic mapping of the region onto a square.*

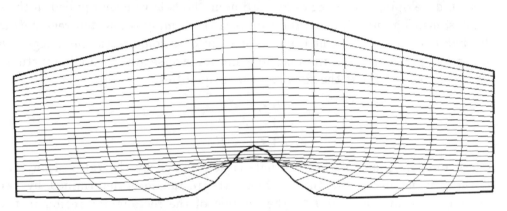

FIG. 2.2. *Grid from the harmonic mapping of a square onto the region.*

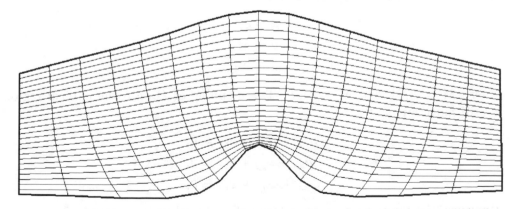

FIG. 2.3. *Grid from the harmonic mapping of a rectangle with approximately the same aspect ratio onto the region.*

in the parametric region for the variables μ and ν, and this system can be inverted to give a system for the parametric variables s and t. The resulting system defined on the square region does not contain the parameter M, but is nonlinear and similar to system (2.4).

The theory behind conformal and elliptic methods for grid generation on surfaces is well developed. However, these methods have not been used extensively due to difficulties encountered with the parameterization of arbitrary surfaces. They have been most successful in generating grids on surfaces defined by analytic equations. Further details on quasi-conformal mappings and conformal mappings on surfaces and their application in grid generation can be found in the paper by Mastin and Thompson [49].

2.3. Three-Dimensional Grid Generation

Although there are no practical conformal mappings for three-dimensional regions, the concepts that have been derived from conformal mappings and used in developing elliptic grid-generation methods have been applied in three dimensions. The principle assumption is that a simply connected region D in the xyz-plane can be mapped one-to-one and onto some rectangular region R of the $\xi\eta\zeta$-plane and that the mapping and its inverse are harmonic functions. The rectangular region is defined by the inequalities

$$0 < \xi < L,$$
$$0 < \eta < W,$$
$$0 < \zeta < H.$$

The geometric shape of the rectangle is determined by the ratio of any two of the dimensions to the third. Thus, the rectangle is determined by two parameters that are similar to the module of the rectangular region in two dimensions. Now, the rectangular region R can be mapped onto the interior of a cube S by the change of variables

$$\mu = \xi,$$
$$\nu = M\eta,$$
$$\omega = N\zeta,$$

where $M = L/W$ and $N = L/H$. The mapping of D onto the cubical region is still harmonic so that

$$\mu_{xx} + \mu_{yy} + \mu_{zz} = 0,$$
$$\nu_{xx} + \nu_{yy} + \nu_{zz} = 0,$$
$$\omega_{xx} + \omega_{yy} + \omega_{zz} = 0.$$

However, the mapping of S onto D satisfies the following system.

$$(2.5) \qquad \begin{aligned} x_{\mu\mu} + M^2 x_{\nu\nu} + N^2 x_{\omega\omega} &= 0, \\ y_{\mu\mu} + M^2 y_{\nu\nu} + N^2 y_{\omega\omega} &= 0, \\ z_{\mu\mu} + M^2 z_{\nu\nu} + N^2 z_{\omega\omega} &= 0. \end{aligned}$$

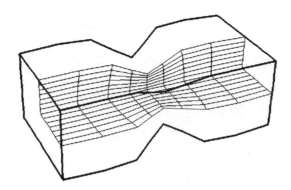

FIG. 2.4. *Grid from the harmonic mapping of the region onto a cube.*

Assuming that the mapping of D onto the rectangular region R preserves aspect ratios of grid cells, the values of M and N can be defined by the following relations:

(2.6)
$$M = \iiint_S \left[\frac{x_\nu^2 + y_\nu^2 + z_\nu^2}{x_\mu^2 + y_\mu^2 + z_\mu^2} \right]^{1/2} d\mu \, d\nu \, d\omega,$$

$$N = \iiint_S \left[\frac{x_\omega^2 + y_\omega^2 + z_\omega^2}{x_\mu^2 + y_\mu^2 + z_\mu^2} \right]^{1/2} d\mu \, d\nu \, d\omega.$$

The results for three dimensions are similar to those for two dimensions. The harmonic mapping of R onto S results in a one-to-one mapping and the grid defined on R does not fold or spill over even for nonconvex regions. This was verified in the paper by Mastin and Thompson [50]. However, the mapping from S onto R, given by solving system (2.5) with Dirichlet boundary conditions, cannot be used for nonconvex regions unless values of M and N can be estimated. This can be demonstrated by considering a simple three-dimensional region. Figure 2.4 is the plot of a grid constructed from a harmonic mapping of R onto S. Figure 2.5 is the plot of a harmonic mapping of S onto R, i.e., a solution of system (2.5) with $M = N = 1$. These values of M and N do not reflect the actual shape of the region R, and as a result the grid folds. A grid constructed with more appropriate values of M and N is plotted in Fig. 2.6. For that grid an initial grid was constructed by interpolation and used to approximate the integrals in equations (2.6). The grids in Figs. 2.4 and 2.6 are almost identical.

2.4. Conclusions

Basic properties of conformal mapping can lead to improved methods of generating grids from the solution of elliptic systems of partial differential equations. In particular, an arbitrary region can be conformally mapped onto a rectangular region, but only if the rectangle has the correct dimensions. The mapping can be scaled to map the region onto a square, or any fixed rectangular

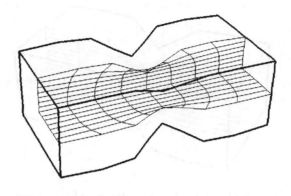

FIG. 2.5. *Grid from the harmonic mapping of a cube onto the region.*

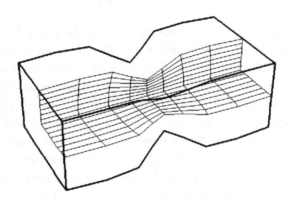

FIG. 2.6. *Grid from the harmonic mapping of a rectangular parallelepiped with approximately the same aspect ratios onto the region.*

region. The scaled mapping of the region onto the square is harmonic, but its inverse is not. This fact should be considered when developing elliptic equations for grid generation. The same is true in three dimensions. The equations for generating the grid must reflect the extent of the region in each of the curvilinear coordinate directions.

2.5. Acknowledgments

This research has been supported by the National Aeronautics and Space Administration (NASA) Langley Research Center under grant NSG–1577.

Chapter 3

Continuum Variational Formulation

J. E. Castillo

3.1. Introduction

In this chapter a rigorous foundation for the variational grid-generation method, introduced by Steinberg and Roache [67], is presented. In §3.2 some standard abstract optimization theory is introduced, and in §3.3 the existence and uniqueness for the smoothness integral are studied using the theory presented in §3.2. In addition, some partial results for the two-dimensional volume integral are presented. Finally, an erroneous result concerning the volume integral that appears in the literature is discussed. In §3.4 the Euler–Lagrange equations for both the smoothness and volume integral are analyzed, and the replication of the reference grid is discussed.

3.2. Optimization and Approximation Topics

The material presented in this section is standard. It is presented on the heels of the developments given in [62]. It is written here to familiarize the reader with the framework in which the variational problems will be studied. The smoothness functional naturally fits in with the general theory; however, the volume functional has some features that make it nontrivial. There is very little theory known about the natural space where the volume functional is well defined. In [11] and [67] the volume integral has been derived from geometrical considerations, and it has not been studied mathematically.

3.2.1. Dirichlet's Principle.

When elliptic boundary-value problems are considered, it is useful to pose them in a weak form [62]. For example, the Dirichlet problem

$$(3.1) \qquad \left. \begin{array}{ll} -\Delta_n u(x) = F(x) , & x \in G , \\ u(s) = 0 , & s \in \partial G \end{array} \right\}$$

on a bounded open set G in $\mathbf{R}^n$, is posed (and solvable) in the following form: Find

$$(3.2) \quad u \in H_0^1(G), \quad \int_G \nabla u \cdot \nabla v \, dx = \int_G F(x) v(x) dx , \quad \text{for all} \quad v \in H_0^1(G) .$$

In the process of formulating certain problems of mathematical physics as boundary-value problems of the type (3.1), integrals of the form appearing in (3.2) arise naturally. Specifically, in describing the displacement $u(x)$ at a point $x \in G$ of a stretched string ($n = 1$) or membrane ($n = 2$) resulting from a unit tension and distributed external force $F(x)$, the potential energy is given by

$$(3.3) \qquad E(u) = \left(\frac{1}{2}\right) \int_G |\nabla u(x)|^2 dx - \int_G F(x)u(x)dx \ .$$

Dirichlet's principle is the statement that the solution u of (3.2) is that function in $H_0^1(G)$ at which the functional $E(\cdot)$ attains its minimum. That is, u is the solution of

$$(3.4) \qquad u \in H_0^1(G) : E(u) \leq E(v) \ , \qquad v \in H_0^1(G) \ .$$

To prove that (3.3) characterizes u, we need only note that for each $v \in H_0^1(G)$,

$$E(u + v) - E(u) = \int_G (\nabla u \cdot \nabla v - Fv)dx + \left(\frac{1}{2}\right) \int_G |\nabla v|^2 dx \ ,$$

and the first term vanishes because of (3.2). Thus $E(u + v) \geq E(u)$, and equality holds only if $v \equiv 0$.

The preceding remarks suggest an alternate proof for the existence of a solution of (3.2); hence, of (3.1). In essence, we seek the element u of $H_0^1(G)$ at which the energy function $E(\cdot)$ attains its minimum, then show that u is the solution of (3.2). We want to minimize functions more general than (3.3) over closed convex subsets of Hilbert space. These more general functions permit us to try to solve some nonlinear elliptic boundary-value problems.

By considering convex sets instead of subspaces, some elementary results on unilateral boundary-value problems are obtained. These arise in applications where the solution is subjected to a one-sided constraint, e.g., $u(x) \geq 0$, and their solutions are characterized by variational inequalities.

3.2.2. Minimization of Convex Functions. Suppose F is a real-valued function defined on a closed interval K (possibly infinite). If F is continuous, and if either K is bounded or $F(x) \to +\infty$ as $|x| \to +\infty$, then F attains its minimum value at some point of K. This result will be extended to certain real-valued functions on Hilbert space and the notions developed will be extremely useful in the remainder of this chapter. An essential point is to characterize the minimum by the derivative of F. Throughout this section, V is a real separable Hilbert space, K is a nonempty subset of V, and $F : K \to \mathbf{R}$ is a function.

The space V is weakly (sequentially) compact [62, §1.6]. It is worthwhile to consider subsets of V that inherit this property. Thus, K is called *weakly (sequentially) closed* if the limit of every weakly convergent sequence from K is contained in K. Since convergence (in norm) implies weak convergence, a weakly closed set is necessarily closed.

LEMMA 3.2.1. *If K is closed and convex (cf. [62, §I.4.2]), then it is weakly closed.*

Proof. Let x be a vector not in K. From Theorem I.4.C of [62], there is an $x_0 \in K$ that is closest to x. By translation, if necessary, we may suppose that $(x_0 + x)/2 = \theta$, i.e., $x = -x_0$. Clearly, $(x, x_0) < 0$, so we need to show that $(z, x_0) \geq 0$ for all $z \in K$; from this the desired result follows easily. Since K is convex, the function $\varphi : [0, 1] \to \mathbf{R}$, given by

$$\varphi(t) = \|(1 - t)x_0 + tz - x\|_V^2 , \qquad 0 \leq t \leq 1 ,$$

has its minimum at $t = 0$. Hence, the right-derivative $\varphi^+(0)$ is nonnegative, i.e.,

$$(x_0 - x, z - x_0) \geq 0 .$$

Since $x = -x_0$, this gives $(x_0, z) \geq \|x_0\|_V^2 > 0$.

The preceding result and Theorem I.6.B of [62] show that each closed, convex, and bounded subset of V is weakly sequentially compact. When considering situations in which K is not bounded (e.g., $K = V$), the following definition is then appropriate.

DEFINITION 3.2.1. The function F has the growth property at $x \in K$ if for some $R > 0$, $y \in K$ and $\|y - x\| \geq R$ implies $F(y) > F(x)$.

The following continuity requirement is adequate for our purposes.

DEFINITION 3.2.2. The function $F : K \to \mathbf{R}$ is weakly lower semicontinuous at $x \in K$ if for every sequence $\{x_n\}$ in K that weakly converges to $x \in K$, we have $F(x) \leq \lim \inf F(x_n)$. (Recall that for any sequence $\{a_n\}$ in $\mathbf{R}$, $\lim \inf(a_n) \equiv \sup_{k \geq 0}(\inf_{n \geq k}(a_n))$.)

THEOREM 3.2.1. *Let K be closed and convex, and $F : K \to \mathbf{R}$ be weakly lower semicontinuous at every point K. If (a) K is bounded or if (b) F has the growth property at some point in K, then there exists an $x_0 \in K$ such that $F(x_0) \leq F(x)$ for all $x \in K$. That is, F attains its minimum on K.*

Proof. Let $m = \inf\{F(x) : x \in K\}$ and $\{x_n\}$ be a sequence in K for which $m = \lim F(x_n)$. If (a) holds, then by weak sequential compactness, there is a subsequence of $\{x_n\}$ denoted by $\{x_{n'}\}$ that converges weakly to $x_0 \in V$, and Lemma 3.2.1 shows $x_0 \in K$. The weak lower semicontinuity of F shows $F(x_0) \leq \lim \inf F(x_{n'}) = m$; hence, $F(x_0) = m$, and the result follows. For the case of (b), let F have the growth property at $z \in K$ and let $R > 0$ be such that $F(x) > F(z)$ whenever $\|z - x\| \geq R$ and $x \in K$. Then set $B \equiv \{x \in V : \|x - z\| \leq R\}$. Now apply (a) to the closed, convex, and bounded set $B \cap K$. The result follows from the observation that $\inf\{F(x) : x \in K\} = \inf\{F(x) : x \in B \cap K\}$.

We note that if K is bounded, then F has the growth property at every point of K; thus, the case (b) of Theorem 3.2.1 includes (a) as a special case. Nevertheless, we prefer to leave Theorem 3.2.1 in its (possibly) more instructive form as given.

The condition that a function be weakly lower semicontinuous is generally difficult to verify. However, for those convex functions (see below), the lower semicontinuity is the same for the weak and strong notions, which can be proved directly from Lemma 3.2.1. We shall consider a class of functions for which convexity and lower semicontinuity are easy to check, and furthermore, this class contains all examples of interest to us here.

DEFINITION 3.2.3. The function $F : K \to \mathbf{R}$ is convex if its domain K is convex, and for all $x, y \in K$ and $t \in [0, 1]$, we have

$$(3.5) \qquad F(tx + (1 - t)y) \leq tF(x) + (1 - t)F(y) \ .$$

DEFINITION 3.2.4. The function $F : K \to \mathbf{R}$ is G-differentiable at $x \in K$ if K is convex and there is an $F'(x) \in V'$ such that

$$\lim_{t \to 0^+} \frac{1}{t}[F(x + t(y - x)) - F(x)] = F'(x)(y - x)$$

for all $y \in K$. $F'(x)$ is called the G-differential of F at x. If F is G-differentiable at every point in K, then $F' : K \to V'$ is the gradient of F on K, and F is the potential of the function F'.

The G-differential $F'(x)$ is precisely the directional derivative of F at the point x in the direction toward y. The following shows how it characterizes convexity of F.

THEOREM 3.2.2. *Let $F : K \to \mathbf{R}$ be G-differentiable on the convex set K. Then the following are equivalent:*

(a) *F is convex.*

(b) *For each pair $x, y \in K$ we have*

$$(3.6) \qquad F'(x)(y - x) \leq F(y) - F(x) \ .$$

(c) *For each pair $x, y \in K$ we have*

$$(3.7) \qquad (F'(x) - F'(y))(x - y) \geq 0 \ .$$

Proof. If F is convex, then $F(x + t(y - x)) \leq F(x) + t(F(y) - F(x))$ for $x, y \in K$ and $t \in [0, 1]$, so (3.6) follows. Thus (a) implies (b).

If (b) holds, we obtain $F'(y)(x - y) \leq F(x) - F(y)$ and $F(x) - F(y) \leq F'(x)(x - y)$, so (c) follows.

Finally, we show that (c) implies (a). Let $x, y \in K$ and define $\varphi : [0, 1] \to \mathbf{R}$ by

$$\varphi(t) = F(tx + (1 - t)y) = F(y + t(x - y)) , \qquad t \in [0, 1] \ .$$

Then $\varphi'(t) = F'(y + t(x - y))(x - y)$ and we have for $0 \leq s < t \leq 1$ the estimate

$$(\varphi'(t) - \varphi'(s))(t - s) = (F'(y + t(x - y))$$
$$-F'(y + s(x - y)))((t - s)(x - y)) \geq 0$$

from (c), so φ' is nondecreasing. The Mean Value Theorem implies that

$$\frac{\varphi(1) - \varphi(t)}{1 - t} \geq \frac{\varphi(t) - \varphi(0)}{t - 0} , \qquad 0 < t < 1 \ .$$

Hence, $\varphi(t) \leq t\varphi(1) + (1 - t)\varphi(0)$, and this is just (3.5).

COROLLARY 3.2.1. *Let F be G-differentiable and convex. Then F is weakly lower semicontinuous on K.*

Proof. Let the sequence $\{x_n\} \subset K$ converge weakly to $x \in K$. Since $F'(x) \in V'$, we have $\lim F'(x)(x_n) = F'(x)(x)$, so from (3.6) we obtain

$$\liminf(F(x_n) - F(x)) \geq \liminf F'(x)(x_n - x) = 0 \ .$$

This shows that F is weakly lower semicontinuous at $x \in K$.

COROLLARY 3.2.2. *In the situation of Corollary 3.2.1, for each pair $x, y \in K$ the function*

$$t \mapsto F'(x + t(y - x))(y - x) \ , \qquad t \in [0,1]$$

is continuous.

Proof. We need only observe that in the proof of Theorem 3.2.2 the function φ' is a monotone derivative and therefore must be continuous.

Our goal is to consider the special case of Theorem 3.2.1 that results when F is a convex potential function. It will be convenient in the applications to have the hypothesis on F stated in terms of its gradient F'.

LEMMA 3.2.2. *Let F be G-differentiable and convex. Suppose also that we have*

$$\lim_{\|x\| \to +\infty} \frac{F'(x)(x)}{\|x\|} = +\infty \ , \qquad x \in K \ .$$

Then $\lim_{\|x\| \to \infty} F(x) = +\infty$, so F has the growth property at every point in K.

Proof. We may assume that $\theta \in K$. For each $x \in K$ we obtain from Corollary 3.2.2

$$F(x) - F(\theta) = \int_0^1 F'(tx)(x)\, dt$$

$$= \int_0^1 (F'(tx) - F'(\theta))(x)\, dt + F'(\theta)(x) \ .$$

With (3.7) this implies

$$(3.8) \qquad F(x) - F(\theta) \geq \int_{1/2}^1 (F'(tx) - F'(\theta))(x)\, dt + F'(\theta)(x) \ .$$

From the Mean Value Theorem it follows that for some $s = s(x) \in \left[\frac{1}{2}, 1\right]$

$$F(x) - F(\theta) \geq (\tfrac{1}{2})(F'(sx)(x) + F'(\theta)(x))$$

$$\geq (\tfrac{1}{2})\|x\| \left\{ \frac{F'(sx)(sx)}{\|sx\|} - \|F'(\theta)\|_{V'} \right\} \ .$$

Since $\|sx\| \geq (\tfrac{1}{2})\|x\|$ for all $x \in K$, the result follows.

DEFINITION 3.2.5. Let D be a nonempty subset of V and let $T : D \to V'$ be a function. Then T is monotone if

$$(T(x) - T(y))(x - y) \geq 0 , \qquad x, y \in D ,$$

and strictly monotone if equality holds only when $x \equiv y$. We call T coercive if

$$\lim_{\|x\| \to \infty} \left(\frac{T(x)(x)}{\|x\|} \right) = +\infty .$$

After the preceding remarks on potential functions, we have the following fundamental results.

THEOREM 3.2.3. *Let K be a nonempty, closed, convex subset of the real separable Hilbert space V, and let the function $F : K \to \mathbf{R}$ be G-differentiable on K. Assume that the gradient F' is monotone and that either* (a) *K is bounded or* (b) *F' is coercive. Then the set $M \equiv \{x \in K : F(x) \leq F(y)$ for all $y \in K\}$ is nonempty, closed, and convex, and $x \in M$ if and only if $x \in K$ and*

$$(3.9) \qquad F'(x)(y - x) \geq 0 , \qquad y \in K .$$

Proof. That M is nonempty follows from Theorems 3.2.1 and 3.2.2, Corollary 3.2.1, and Lemma 3.2.1. Each of the sets $M_y \equiv \{x \in K : F(x) \leq F(y)\}$ is closed and convex so their intersection, M, is closed and convex. If $x \subset M$, then (3.9) follows from the definition of $F'(x)$; conversely, (3.6) shows that (3.9) implies $x \in M$.

We close with a sufficient condition for uniqueness of the minimum point.

DEFINITION 3.2.6. The function $F : K \to \mathbf{R}$ is strictly convex if its domain is convex and for $x, y \in K$, $x \neq y$, and $t \in (0, 1)$, we have

$$F(tx + (1 - t)y) < tF(x) + (1 - t)F(y) .$$

THEOREM 3.2.4. *A strictly convex function $F : K \to \mathbf{R}$ has at most one point at which the minimum is attained.*

Proof. Suppose $x_1, x_2 \in K$ with $F(x_1) = F(x_2) = \inf\{F(y) : y \in K\}$, and $x_1 \neq x_2$. Since $\frac{1}{2}(x_1 + x_2) \in K$, the strict convexity of F gives

$$F\left((\tfrac{1}{2})(x_1 + x_2)\right) < (\tfrac{1}{2})(F(x_1) + F(x_2)) = \inf\{F(y) : y \in K\} ,$$

and this is a contradiction.

The third part of the proof of Theorem 3.2.2 gives the following theorem.

THEOREM 3.2.5. *Let F be G-differentiable on K. If the gradient F' is strictly monotone, then F is strictly convex.*

3.2.3. Variational Inequalities. The characterization (3.9) of the minimum point u of F on K is an example of a *variational inequality*. It expresses the fact that from the minimum point the function does not decrease in any direction into the set K. Moreover, if the minimum point is an interior point of K, then we obtain the *variational equality* $F'(u) = 0$, a functional equation for the (gradient) operator F'.

We shall write out the special form of the preceding results, which occur when F is a quadratic function. Thus, V is a real Hilbert space, $f \in V'$, and $a(\cdot, \cdot): V \times V \to \mathbf{R}$ is continuous, bilinear, and symmetric. Define $F: V \to \mathbf{R}$ by

$$(3.10) \qquad F(v) = \left(\tfrac{1}{2}\right) a(v, v) - f(v), \qquad v \in V.$$

From the symmetry of $a(\cdot, \cdot)$ we find that the G-differential of F is given by

$$F'(u)(v - u) = a(u, v - u) - f(v - u), \qquad u, v \in V.$$

If $\mathcal{A}: V \to V'$ is the operator characterizing the form $a(\cdot, \cdot)$ (cf. [62, §1.5.4]), then we obtain

$$(3.11) \qquad F'(u) = \mathcal{A}u - f, \qquad u \in V.$$

To check the convexity of F by the monotonicity of its gradient, we compute

$$(F'u - F'v)(u - v) = a(u - v, u - v) = \mathcal{A}(u - v)(u - v).$$

Thus, F' is monotone (strictly monotone) exactly when $a(\cdot, \cdot)$ is nonnegative (respectively, positive), and this is equivalent to $\mathcal{A}$ being monotone (respectively, positive) (cf. [62, §V.2]). The growth of F is implied by the statement

$$(3.12) \qquad \lim_{\|v\| \to \infty} \left(\frac{a(v, v)}{\|v\|} \right) = +\infty.$$

Since $F(v) \geq (\tfrac{1}{2}a(v, v)) - \|f\| \cdot \|v\|$, from the identity (3.11) we find that (3.12) is equivalent to F' being coercive.

The preceding remarks show that Theorems 3.2.3 and 3.2.4 give the following theorem.

THEOREM 3.2.6. *Let* $a(\cdot, \cdot) : V \times V \to \mathbf{R}$ *be continuous, bilinear, symmetric, and nonnegative. Suppose* $f \in V'$ *and* K *is a closed, convex subset of* V. *Assume that either* (a) K *is bounded or* (b) $a(\cdot, \cdot)$ *is* V-*coercive. Then there exists a* $u \in K$ *that satisfies*

$$(3.13) \qquad a(u, v - u) \geq f(v - u), \qquad v \in K.$$

There is exactly one such u *in the case of* (b), *and there is exactly one in case* (a) *if we further assume that* $a(\cdot, \cdot)$ *is positive.*

Finally, we note that when K is the whole space V, then (3.13) is equivalent to

$$(3.14) \qquad a(u, v) = f(v), \qquad v \in V.$$

For this reason, when (3.14) is equivalent to a boundary-value problem, it is called the variational form of that problem, and such problems are called variational boundary-value problems.

3.3. Variational Integrals

In the variational methods introduced by Steinberg and Roache [67], two functionals are presented that provide (1) the measure of spacing between the grid lines (smoothness) and (2) the measure of the area of the grid cells. The minimization problem is usually solved by calculating the Euler–Lagrange (E–L) equations for the variational problem. The computer creates a grid by solving a central finite-difference approximation of the E–L equations. A reference grid is used to place the grid properties on the boundary as well as on the interior [67].

In m dimensions the integrals to be minimized are, for smoothness,

$$(3.15) \qquad I_s = \int_B \sum_{j=1}^m \left[\frac{\left\| \frac{\partial \vec{u}}{\partial \nu_j} \right\|^2}{\left\| \frac{\partial \vec{\tau}}{\partial \nu_j} \right\|} \right] |d\vec{\nu}|,$$

with

$$(3.16) \qquad C_s = \int_B \sum_{i=1}^m \sum_{j=1}^m \frac{\partial u_i}{\partial \nu_j} |\partial \vec{\nu}| = \text{ constant};$$

and for volume (area),

$$(3.17) \qquad I_v = \int_B \frac{J^2 \begin{bmatrix} \vec{u} \\ \vec{\nu} \end{bmatrix}}{J \begin{bmatrix} \vec{\tau} \\ \vec{\nu} \end{bmatrix}} |d\vec{\nu}|,$$

with

$$(3.18) \qquad C_v = \int_B J \begin{bmatrix} \vec{u} \\ \vec{\nu} \end{bmatrix} |d\vec{\nu}| = \text{ constant}.$$

Here

$$\vec{u} = (u_1, u_2, \cdots, u_m) ,$$
$$\vec{\nu} = (\nu_1, \nu_2, \cdots, \nu_m) ,$$
$$\vec{\tau} = (\tau_1, \tau_2, \cdots, \tau_m) ,$$
$$\vec{u} = \vec{u}(\vec{\nu}) ,$$
$$\vec{\tau} = \vec{\tau}(\vec{\nu}) ,$$
$$|d\vec{\nu}| = d\nu_1 d\nu_2 \cdots d\nu_m ,$$

and B is a "box" in $\vec{\tau}$ space. Also $\vec{\tau}$ is a given map from B to the reference region. $\vec{u}$ maps B onto the physical region G; it is given on the boundary and must be calculated in the interior of the region. Also

$$J \begin{bmatrix} \vec{u} \\ \vec{\nu} \end{bmatrix}$$

is the Jacobian of the mapping $\vec{u}$ of the logical space to physical space and

$$J \begin{bmatrix} \vec{\tau} \\ \vec{\nu} \end{bmatrix}$$

is the Jacobian of the reference mapping. In this case the constraints are automatically satisfied [67]. In general, we are interested in minimizing a weighted combination of the two integrals

$$(3.19) \qquad I = \sigma I_s + (1 - \sigma)I_v \,,$$

with the constraint

$$(3.20) \qquad \sigma \geq 0 \,.$$

The variational problem we are interested in is the minimization of the integral I, with the reference grid set to be equal to the unit square, which is the same as the logical region, over the class of all proper mappings of B to G, with a fixed value on the boundary of B. A region is a subset of a Euclidean space that is connected, and it is the closure of an open set. Moreover, the boundary should consist of a finite number of smooth pieces. A function is smooth if it is infinitely differentiable in the region where it is defined and continuous up to and including the boundary of the region. A proper mapping of region B to region G is a smooth mapping that is defined on all of B and is one-to-one and onto G (see [67]).

3.3.1. Smoothness Integral. In the case of $\sigma = 1$, we have the pure smoothness problem. This problem can be stated in abstract form as follows: Find $\vec{u} \in K$ such that

$$(3.21) \qquad F(\vec{u}) \leq F(\vec{v}) \,, \qquad \vec{v} \in K.$$

Here $K = \{\vec{u_0} + \vec{u}, \vec{u_0} \in H_0^1 \text{ and } \vec{u} \in H^1\}$ and

$$(3.22) \qquad F(\vec{u}) = \int_B \sum_{i=1}^m \|\nabla \vec{u_i}\|^2 |d\vec{v}| \,.$$

Here K is closed and convex and the following claims will characterize the functional F.

Claim 3.1. F is G-differentiable.

Proof.

$$(3.23) \qquad F'(\vec{u})(\vec{v} - \vec{u}) = \lim_{t \to 0^+} \frac{F(\vec{u} + t(\vec{v} - \vec{u})) - F(\vec{u})}{t} = 2 \int_B \sum_{i=1}^m \langle \nabla \vec{u_i}, \nabla(\vec{v_i} - \vec{u_i}) \rangle \,.$$

Claim 3.2. F' is strictly monotonic.

Proof.

$$(3.24) \qquad F'(\vec{u})(\vec{v} - \vec{u}) = 2 \int_B \sum_{i=1}^m \langle \nabla \vec{u_i}, \nabla(\vec{v_i} - \vec{u_i}) \rangle;$$

hence,

$$(3.25) \qquad (F'(\vec{u}) - F'(\vec{v}))(\vec{u} - \vec{v}) = 2 \int_B \sum_{i=1}^m \langle \nabla(\vec{u_i} - \vec{v_i}), \nabla(\vec{u_i} - \vec{v_i}) \rangle \quad \geq 0$$

and 0 only if $u \equiv v$. The following classical result will be useful in the next claim.

LEMMA 3.3.1 (Poincaré Inequality). *Let $\vec{u_0} \in H_0^1$; then*

$$(3.26) \qquad \|\vec{u_0}\| \le C\|\nabla\vec{u_0}\| .$$

Claim 3.3. F' is coercive.

Proof. Let $\vec{u} = \vec{u_0} + \vec{v}$, $\vec{v} \in H^1$, $\vec{u_0} \in H_0^1$:

$$
\begin{aligned}
\frac{F'(\vec{u})(\vec{u})}{\|\vec{u}\|_{H^1}} &= \frac{2\|\nabla\vec{u}\|_2^2}{\|\vec{u}\|_2 + \|\nabla\vec{u}\|_2} \\
&= \frac{2\|\nabla\vec{u_0} + \nabla\vec{v}\|_2^2}{\|\vec{u_0} + \vec{v}\|_2 + \|\nabla\vec{u_0} + \nabla\vec{v}\|_2} \\
&\ge \frac{2\|\nabla\vec{u_0}\|_2^2}{\|\vec{u_0}\|_2 + \|\nabla\vec{u_0}\|_2 + K} \\
&\ge \frac{2\|\nabla\vec{u_0}\|_2^2}{(C+1)\|\nabla\vec{u_0}\|_2 + K} \\
&\ge \|\nabla\vec{u_0}\|_2 \to \infty \text{ as } \|\vec{u_0}\|_{H_1^0} \to \infty.
\end{aligned}
$$

The three previous claims are the proof of the following theorem.

THEOREM 3.3.1. *The smoothness integral has a unique minimum.*

Proof. F is G-differentiable on a nonempty, closed, and convex set K; F' is strictly monotonic; and F' is coercive. Therefore, (by Theorem 3.2.3) F has a unique minimum.

We can also look at the Hessian of the smoothness functional.

Claim 3.4. The Hessian of the smoothness integral is positive definite.

Proof. Set $\vec{u} = (u_1, \cdots, u_m)$, $\vec{h} = (h_1, h_2, \cdots, h_m)$, $\vec{w} = (w_1, w_2, \cdots, w_m)$, then

$$F(\vec{u}) = \int_B \sum_{j=1}^m \left\|\frac{\partial\vec{u}}{\partial v_j}\right\|^2 ,$$

$$F(\vec{u}) = \int_B \sum_{j=1}^m (\nabla u_j)^2,$$

$$F'(\vec{u})(\vec{h}) = 2\int_B (\nabla u_1, \cdots, \nabla u_m) \cdot (h_1, \cdots, h_m)^t,$$

$$F''(\vec{u})(\vec{h})(\vec{w}) = \int_B (w_1, w_2, \cdots, w_m)$$

$$\begin{pmatrix} \nabla^2 u_1 & 0 & \cdots & 0 \\ 0 & \nabla^2 u_2 & 0 & \cdots \\ 0 & & \cdots & 0 & \nabla^2 u_m \end{pmatrix} (h_1 \cdots h_m)^t \ge 0 ,$$

so clearly the Hessian of the smoothness functional is positive definite.

3.3.2. Volume Integral in Two Dimensions.

The standard theory introduced at the beginning of this chapter provided us with the natural framework for the study of the pure smoothness problem; in fact, the proof that the smoothness functional has a unique minimum is a direct result of applying a standard technique. The volume problem, on the other hand, does not fit into any standard technique. This makes the volume problem more exciting and also harder to study. The problem of existence of a unique minimum is by no means solved here. It will remain an open problem until enough theoretical results are developed in the Sobolev space W_1^4, the natural space where the volume functional is well defined. Some partial results are given in order to gain some insight into the behavior of the volume functional. The main problem with the volume integral is that its natural space is W_1^4. Since there are not presently enough results for functionals on this space, it is not possible at this time to extend the techniques used for the smoothness case. A complete study of W_1^4 is beyond this work. However, some partial results are presented in order to get a better understanding of the behavior of the volume integral.

Claim 3.5. If $J(u) > 0$ (the Jacobian of the mapping u), then the formal Hessian of the volume functional is positive definite. Let

$$F(u) = \int_B J^2 \begin{pmatrix} x & y \\ \xi & \eta \end{pmatrix} d\xi d\eta \,,$$

then,

$$F(u + \epsilon h) = \int_B J^2 \begin{pmatrix} x + \epsilon a & y + \epsilon b \\ \xi & \eta \end{pmatrix} d\xi d\eta \,;$$

hence,

$$\left. \frac{dF}{d\epsilon} \right|_{\epsilon=0} = 2 \int_B J \begin{pmatrix} x & y \\ \xi & \eta \end{pmatrix} \left[J \begin{pmatrix} a & y \\ \xi & \eta \end{pmatrix} + J \begin{pmatrix} x & b \\ \xi & \eta \end{pmatrix} \right] d\xi d\eta \,,$$

and

$$\left. \frac{d^2 F}{d\epsilon^2} \right|_{\epsilon=0} = \int_B \left[J \begin{pmatrix} a & y \\ \xi & \eta \end{pmatrix} + J \begin{pmatrix} x & b \\ \xi & \eta \end{pmatrix} \right]^2$$
$$+ 2J \begin{pmatrix} x & y \\ \xi & \eta \end{pmatrix} J \begin{pmatrix} a & b \\ \xi & \eta \end{pmatrix} \geq 0 \,.$$

Here the expression for the second derivative is obtained after some algebraic manipulations.

There also exists computer experience with the volume integral for some model problems we have worked with. The previous result plus some computational experience, [22] and [20], give us some evidence for the following conjecture.

Conjecture. If $J(u) \geq 0$ (the Jacobian of the mapping u), then the minimum of I_v has a unique solution.

Steinberg and Roache [67] claim that the volume integral produces grid cells as close as possible to having constant area. A result in two dimensions presented here agrees with their intuitive claim.

THEOREM 3.3.2. *If the Jacobian of the mapping* u, $J(u) \geq 0$, *then the volume integral produces grid cells of constant area* [52].

Proof. Let $\vec{u} = (x, y)$ and $\vec{v} = (\xi, \eta)$ and

$$(3.27) \qquad F(u) = \int_B (x_\xi y_\eta - x_\eta y_\xi)^2 \ .$$

The Euler–Lagrange equations for the volume integral in two dimensions can be computed from the previous formulas using integration by parts. The general formulas are recorded in § 3.4; for this case they are

$$y_\xi J_\eta - y_\eta J_\xi = 0 \ ,$$
$$x_\xi J_\eta - x_\eta J_\xi = 0 \ .$$

The coefficient matrix is the Jacobian of the mapping $\vec{u}$. Hence, if $J \neq 0 \Rightarrow J =$ constant.

3.3.3. An Example of Volume-Preserving Maps in Two Dimensions.

In the process of analyzing the volume integral, it will be helpful to clarify a claim that appears in the literature but that is not applicable to the problem in which we are interested. Brackbill and Saltzman [11, p. 345] state that the volume integral cannot be minimized by itself and that it has an infinite number of solutions. In order to understand their claim a little better, we will look at their problem.

Let Ω be any region in the (x, y) plane. Suppose that $x_0(\xi, \eta)$, $y_0(\xi, \eta)$ with Jacobian J_0 minimizes I_v. A family of mappings from Ω to Ω :

$$x = x(t, x_0, y_0), \qquad y = y(t, x_0, y_0)$$

is constructed. They solve the following problem:

$$\nabla^2 \psi = 0 \ , \qquad \vec{n} \cdot \nabla \psi = 0 \ , \qquad \psi = \psi(x, y) \quad \text{in} \quad \Omega \ .$$

Now let

$$(u(x, y), v(x, y)) = \nabla_{xy} \psi$$

and solve the following autonomous system of ordinary differential equations:

$$\frac{\partial x}{\partial t}(t, x_0, y_0) = u(x(t, x_0, y_0), y(t, x_0, y_0)) \ , \qquad x(0) = x_0 \ ,$$

$$\frac{\partial y}{\partial t}(t, x_0, y_0) = v(x, (t, x_0, y_0), y(t, x_0, y_0)) \ , \qquad y(0) = y_0 \ .$$

The Jacobian of the map $(x_0, y_0) \Rightarrow (x, y)$ is

$$J = \frac{\partial x}{\partial x_0}(t, x_0, y_0) \frac{\partial y}{\partial y_0}(t, x_0, y_0) - \frac{\partial x}{\partial y_0}(t, x_0, y_0) \frac{\partial y}{\partial x_0}(t, x_0, y_0) \ .$$

Now since $x_t = u$ and $y_t = v$, the chain rule gives

$$\frac{1}{J}\frac{\partial J}{\partial t} = \frac{\partial u}{\partial x} + \frac{\partial v}{\partial y} \, .$$

Since $\text{div}(u, v) = 0$, then $J_t = 0$. At $t = 0$ the map $(x_0, y_0) \Rightarrow (x, y)$ is the identity, so $J \equiv 1$ for all t. Thus, the mapping $(\xi, \eta) \Rightarrow (x, y)$ has constant J. Hence, all of these maps minimize I_v. However, we note that this is a problem in which the boundary values are not fixed. Since the problem we are interested in has the boundary values fixed, we can see that the Brackbill and Saltzman claim does not apply to the volume integral we are considering for the grid-generation problem.

3.4. Euler–Lagrange Equations in Two Dimensions

In the case $m = 2$, we set

$$\vec{u} = (x, y) \, , \qquad \vec{v} = (\xi, n) \, , \qquad \vec{\tau} = (\alpha, \beta) \, .$$

Hence, the integral to be minimized for smoothness is

$$I_s = \int_B \frac{x_\xi^2 + y_\xi^2 + x_\eta^2 + y_\eta^2}{(\alpha_\xi^2 + \beta_\eta^2 + \alpha_\eta^2 + \beta_\xi^2)^{1/2}} d\xi d\eta \, ,$$

and for volume,

$$I_v = \int_B \frac{(x_\xi y_\eta - x_\eta y_\xi)^2}{(\alpha_\xi \beta_\eta - \alpha_\eta \beta_\xi)} d\xi d\eta \, ,$$

and then the E–L equations [17] for the smoothness are:

$$
\begin{aligned}
\frac{1}{A} x_{\xi\xi} + \frac{1}{B} x_{\eta\eta} &= \frac{x_\xi A_\xi}{A^2} + \frac{x_\eta B_\eta}{B^2} \, , \\
\frac{1}{A} y_{\xi\xi} + \frac{1}{B} y_{\eta\eta} &= \frac{y_\xi A_\xi}{A^2} + \frac{y_\eta B_\eta}{B^2} \, ,
\end{aligned}
$$

(3.28)

where

$$A = (\alpha_\xi^2 + \beta_\xi^2)^{1/2} \, , \qquad B = (\alpha_\eta^2 + \beta_\eta^2)^{1/2} \, ,$$

and

$$A_\xi = \frac{\alpha_\xi \alpha_{\xi\xi} + \beta_\xi \beta_{\xi\xi}}{A} \, , \qquad B_\eta = \frac{\alpha_\eta \alpha_{\eta\eta} + \beta_\eta \beta_{\eta\eta}}{B} \, .$$

The E–L equations [17] for the volume are:

(3.29)
$$
\begin{aligned}
J[(J_R)_\xi y_\eta - (J_R)_\eta y_\xi] + (J_R)[y_\xi J_\eta - y_\eta J_\xi] &= 0 \, , \\
J[-(J_R)_\xi x_\eta + (J_R)_\eta x_\xi] + (J_R)[x_\eta J_\xi - x_\xi J_\eta] &= 0 \, ,
\end{aligned}
$$

where J_R is the Jacobian of the reference mapping $\vec{\tau}$ and J is the Jacobian of the mapping we want to construct. For the smoothness problem, A and B are fixed and positive if the reference map is proper. The E–L equations are linear, elliptic, and uncoupled. Note that this is as true for m dimensions as it is for two dimensions.

The E–L equations for the volume problem can also be written in the following way:

$$b_{v1}x_{\xi\xi} + b_{v2}x_{\xi\eta} + b_{v3}x_{\eta\eta} + a_{v1}y_{\xi\xi} + a_{v2}y_{\xi\eta} + a_{v3}y_{\eta\eta} = \frac{((J_R)_\eta y_\xi - (J_R)_\xi y_\eta)J}{J_R},$$

$$a_{v1}x_{\xi\xi} + a_{v2}x_{\xi\eta} + a_{v3}x_{\eta\eta} + c_{v1}y_{\xi\xi} + c_{v2}y_{\xi\eta} + c_{v3}y_{\eta\eta} = \frac{((J_R)_\xi x_\eta - (J_R)_\eta x_\xi)J}{J_R},$$

where

$$\begin{aligned}
a_{v1} &= -x_\eta y_\eta, & b_{v1} &= y_\eta^2, & c_{v1} &= x_\eta^2, \\
a_{v2} &= x_\xi y_\eta + x_\eta y_\xi, & b_{v2} &= -2y_\xi y_\eta, & c_{v2} &= -2x_\xi x_\eta, \\
a_{v3} &= -x_\xi y_\xi, & b_{v3} &= y_\xi^2, & c_{v3} &= x_\xi^2.
\end{aligned}$$

It will be shown that these equations are nonlinear, not elliptic, and coupled. To see this situation more clearly, we now do an analysis for the simplest form of these equations [17].

3.4.1. Near-Identity Analysis in Two Dimensions.

In order to study solutions of the E–L equations that are nearly identity maps, $x = \xi$ and $y = \eta$, the reference map is chosen to be the identity. To do a near-identity analysis we view the E–L equations as quasi-linear partial differential equations (PDEs) of the form

$$Af_{\xi\xi} + Bf_{\xi\eta} + Cf_{\eta\eta} = D,$$

where A, B, C, D depend on f, f_ξ, f_η. Here A, B, C, D are made constant by choosing fixed f, f_ξ, f_η.

To study near-identity maps, set $x = \xi$, $y = \eta$, so $x_\xi = 1$, $x_\eta = 0$, $y_\xi = 0$, and $y_\eta = 1$. The E–L equations for the smoothness integral become

$$(3.30) \qquad x_{\xi\xi} + x_{\eta\eta} = 0, \qquad y_{\xi\xi} + y_{\eta\eta} = 0,$$

which is an uncoupled elliptic system of PDEs. However, in the case of the volume integral, we get a degenerate system,

$$(3.31) \qquad x_{\xi\xi} + y_{\xi\eta} = 0, \qquad x_{\xi\eta} + y_{\eta\eta} = 0,$$

which can be easily checked to be nonelliptic.

Based on this, we should expect difficulties with the codes that are used for solving these problems, since they are elliptic solvers. Nevertheless, experience shows the opposite to be the case (see [17], [20], and [67]).

3.4.2. Replication of Reference Grid Properties in Two Dimensions.

One of the questions to be asked with respect to the usefulness of the reference grid concept is, "Is it possible to reproduce any reference grid on the physical object?" The simplest test of the replication property can be applied by choosing the reference region to be the same as the physical region, and checking to see if the reference mapping satisfies the Euler–Lagrange equations. However, we do not expect an arbitrary reference grid to be replicated and indeed, this did not happen. When we choose the mapping, $x = \alpha$, $y = \beta$, the smoothness equations for (x, y) become

$$C_1 \alpha_{\xi\xi} + C_2 \alpha_{\eta\eta} + C_3 \beta_{\xi\xi} + C_4 \beta_{\eta\eta} = 0,$$
$$-C_3 \alpha_{\xi\xi} + C_4 \alpha_{\eta\eta} + D_3 \beta_{\xi\xi} + D_4 \beta_{\eta\eta} = 0,$$

where

$$C_1 = B^3 \beta_\xi^2, \qquad C_4 = -A^3 \alpha_\eta \beta_\eta,$$
$$C_2 = A^3 \beta_\eta^2, \qquad D_3 = -B^3 \alpha_\xi^2,$$
$$C_3 = -B^3 \alpha_\xi B_\xi, \quad D_4 = -A^3 \alpha_\eta^2,$$

with

$$A = (\alpha_\xi^2 + \beta_\xi^2)^{1/2}, \qquad B = (\alpha_\eta^2 + \beta_\eta^2)^{1/2}.$$

Since generally these equations are nontrivial, it is not possible to replicate the reference grid except in simple geometries. In particular, if the reference grid is a quadrilateral, x and y are linear; hence, the above equations are satisfied, so the smoothness integral replicates the reference grid. In the case of the volume control, a similar calculation can be done. After some algebra, the constraining equations become an identity.

3.5. Conclusions

The variational grid-generation method introduced by Steinberg and Roache [67] produces grids suitable for numerical calculations. The volume functional properly combined with the smoothness functional is enough to produce reasonable grids. The Euler–Lagrange equations associated with the smoothness functional are linear, uncoupled, and elliptic; this is not the case for the volume functional in which the Euler–Lagrange equations are nonlinear, coupled, and also not always elliptic. The reference grid concept is a useful tool for exercising more refined control over the grid. It is possible to replicate simple reference grids; it is also useful in preventing the grid from folding [18].

Standard variational techniques were used to completely characterize the smoothness functional; the volume functional, on the other hand, is a very difficult problem. It is partially characterized in this chapter and some results that are helpful in understanding the method have also been presented.

Chapter 4

Discrete Variational Grid Generation

J. E. Castillo

4.1. Introduction

In the variational methods introduced by Steinberg and Roache [67], which are similar to those introduced by Brackbill and Saltzman [11], three functionals are presented that provide a measure of spacing between the grid lines (smoothness), a measure of the area of the grid cells, and the orthogonality of the grid lines. The minimization problem is usually solved by calculating the Euler–Lagrange (E–L) equations for the variational problem and a grid is created by solving a centered finite-difference approximation of these equations. In theory, a straightforward discretization of the integrals should provide a similar solution; instead, there are serious difficulties [16]. In the present approach, the derivatives in the integrals are replaced by centered finite differences, and the integrals are replaced by summations over the gridpoints. Only first derivatives of the coordinates appear in the direct minimization problem, so a centered finite-difference discretization at a gridpoint does not involve values at that point. This produces strong decoupling problems for the direct approach, none of which are manifested in the E–L approach. (See [42].)

In the E–L formulation [67], there are certain integral constraints on the solution that are automatically satisfied. In the straightforward direct formulation, the analogue of these constraints is not automatically satisfied. The straightforward discretization approach transforms the smoothness integral into a linear minimization problem with a linear constraint, while the area integral is transformed into a nonlinear minimization problem with a nonlinear constraint [16]. Such problems are much harder to solve than the unconstrained problems that occur in the continuous cases. A better formulation of the variational grid-generation method, called the "direct" formulation, is obtained when the properties to be controlled are derived directly from the discrete geometry [15], [19]. This method will be described below. While there have been other efforts in generating grids by the optimization of direct properties (see Kennon and Dulikravich [42]), the functionals for the method presented here, as well as its properties and the minimization procedure used, differ considerably.

As in the E–L approach, the direct approach controls three properties of the grid: grid spacing, grid cell area, and grid orthogonality. The grid spacing and cell area functionals have been studied in [19] and [13]. The effects of adding orthogonality control are presented in [14]. To make this paper self-contained, all three functionals will be described below; more detail and analysis can be found in [19] and [13]. In order to understand the behavior of the direct variational method, it is important to understand the behavior of each functional separately. A good comprehension of the solution of each minimization problem will provide information relevant to the more general minimization problem that is being considered, i.e., a weighted combination of the three functionals. In §4.2, an intuitive description of the functionals is given, followed by the notation and a more detailed presentation of the functionals, along with a brief discussion about the minimization procedures and their performance. In §4.3, it is proved that the discrete length control provides the optimal grid produced by the continuous length control functional as a limit case. Finally, in §4.4, a model problem for the area functional is presented to demonstrate the effect of the boundary on the existence and uniqueness of equal area solutions for the area functional.

4.2. Review

4.2.1. Direct Variational Formulation in Two Dimensions.
The simplest length control is given by trying, in a variational sense, to make the grid segments equal. To do this, the sum of the squares of the segment lengths between the gridpoints should be minimized: Let s_{ij} be the length between the (i, j) gridpoint and any neighboring gridpoint, then

$$\text{(4.1)} \qquad \text{minimize } F_S = \sum s_{ij}^2$$

with the constraint (see [67])

$$\text{(4.2)} \qquad C_S = \sum s_{ij} = \text{constant.}$$

For controlling the area of the cells, the sum of the squares of the true discrete area of the quadrilateral cell should be minimized: Let A_{ij} be the area of the (i, j) grid cell, and then

$$\text{(4.3)} \qquad \text{minimize } F_A = \sum A_{ij}^2,$$

with the constraint

$$\text{(4.4)} \qquad C_A = \sum A_{ij} = \text{constant.}$$

For controlling the angles between grid lines, the following functional should be minimized: Let O_{ij} be the dot product of two vectors with origin at the (i, j) gridpoint and then

$$\text{(4.5)} \qquad \text{minimize } F_O = \sum O_{ij}^2$$

with no constraint.

It is worth noting that in this direct variational approach for spacing between the grid lines, the constraint is automatically satisfied, since the sum of all the segments is a telescopic sum which depends only on the values on the boundary (see [7], [19], and [13]). For the area sum, the constraint is the sum of the areas of the true quadrilateral cells, which is shown to be the total area of the region, and solely depends on the values on the boundary (see [7], [19], and [13]). There is no constraint for the orthogonality functional [67] (and one is not needed).

To control all three properties, a weighted combination of all the sums is to be minimized:

(4.6) $$F = aF_S + bF_A + cF_O ,$$

where a, b, and c are given numbers such that

(4.7) $$a + b + c = 1, \qquad a \geq 0, \qquad b \geq 0, \qquad c \geq 0 .$$

4.2.2. Notation. The following notation is used (see [7], [15], and [19]). A given region $\Omega \subset \mathbf{R}^2$ is polygonal if the boundary of Ω is the union of simple closed polygons. A grid on a polygonal region Ω is a subdivision of Ω into quadrilaterals, the vertices of the quadrilaterals are called the points of the grid, and the quadrilaterals are called the cells of the grid. The region will have $m + 2$ points in the logical "horizontal" direction (m interior points) and $n+2$ points in the logical "vertical" direction (n interior) points; hence, the grid has mn interior points. Let $P_{ij} = (x_{ij}, y_{ij})^t$, $2 \leq i \leq m$, and $2 \leq j \leq n$ be the (i, j) point. A column vector of all the $2mn$ coordinates of the mn interior points is needed, so let z be the column vector formed with the coordinates of the interior points; i.e., if $P_{r,s} = (x_{r,s}, y_{r,s})$, then

$$z^t = (x_{2,2}, y_{2,2}, x_{2,3}, y_{2,3}, \cdots, x_{m+1,n+1}, y_{m+1,n+1})$$

and z is of order $2mn$. The grid has $m+2$ points on each "horizontal" boundary and $n + 2$ points on each "vertical" boundary. The points on the "horizontal" boundaries are

$$\{P_{1,1}, P_{2,1}, P_{3,1}, \cdots, P_{m+1,1}, P_{m+2,1}\}$$

and

$$\{P_{1,m+2}, P_{2,m+2}, P_{3,m+2}, \cdots, P_{m+1,n+2}, P_{m+2,n+2}\} .$$

Similarly, the points on the "vertical" boundary are

$$\{P_{1,1}, P_{1,2}, P_{1,3}, \cdots, P_{1,n+1}, P_{1,n+2}\}$$

and

$$\{P_{m+2,1}, P_{m+2,2}, P_{m+2,3}, \cdots, P_{m+2,n+1}, P_{m+2,n+2}\} .$$

The mn interior points are

$$\{P_{2,2}, \quad P_{2,3}, \quad \cdots, \quad P_{2,n+1},$$
$$P_{3,2}, \quad P_{3,3}, \quad \cdots, \quad P_{3,n+1},$$
$$\vdots$$
$$P_{m+1,2}, \quad P_{m+1,3}, \quad \cdots, \quad P_{m+1,n+1}\}.$$

4.2.3. Grid Spacing Control. In order to control the lengths of the logical "horizontal" segments between the gridpoints, consider the functional S_H given by

$$(4.8) \qquad S_H = \sum_{i=1}^{m+1} \sum_{j=2}^{n+1} \ell_{ij}^2, \qquad \ell_{ij} = \|P_{i+1,j} - P_{i,j}\|_2,$$

where ℓ_{ij} are the lengths of the logical "horizontal" segments. Similarly, consider the functional S_V given by

$$(4.9) \qquad S_V = \sum_{i=2}^{m+1} \sum_{j=1}^{n+1} \tilde{\ell}_{ij}^2, \qquad \tilde{\ell}_{ij} = \|P_{i,j+1} - P_{ij}\|_2,$$

which allows the lengths of the "vertical" segments between the points of the grid to be controlled. Hence, the functional F_S can be written

$$(4.10) \qquad F_S(z) = S_H(z) + S_V(z).$$

4.2.4. Functional F_A for Area Control. Let F_A denote the sum of the squares of the area of the grid cells; i.e.,

$$(4.11) \qquad F_A = \sum_{i=1}^{m+1} \sum_{j=1}^{n+1} A_{i,j}^2,$$

where $A_{i,j}$ is the area of the (i,j)th cell. F_A will permit control of the area of the cells. In order to be precise, the (i,j)th cell of the grid is the "oriented quadrilateral," $P_{i,j}, P_{i+1,j}, P_{i+1,j+1}, P_{i,j+1}$. It is important to notice that there are $(m+1)(n+1)$ areas and that there are mn interior points in the grid; that is, there are $2mn$ unknown grid coordinates. Let a be the column vector of order $(m+1)(n+1)$ whose components are the areas of the cells of the grid; i.e.,

$$a^t = (A_{1,1}, A_{1,2}, \cdots, A_{1,n+1}, A_{2,1}, A_{2,2}, \cdots, A_{2,n+1}, \cdots, A_{m+1,1}, \cdots, A_{m+1,n+1}),$$

where

$$A_{ij} = (\tfrac{1}{2})\det(P_{ij} - P_{i+1,j+1}, P_{i+1,j} - P_{i,j+1});$$

then, the functional can be written as

$$(4.12) \qquad F_A = \|a\|_2^2.$$

4.2.5. Functional F_O for Orthogonality Control. There are four angles in each grid cell: upper right, upper left, lower left, and lower right. In order to control the orthogonality of the logical "upper right" angles between the grid lines, consider the functional O_{UR} given by

$$(4.13) \quad O_{UR} = \sum_i \sum_j O_{ij}^2 , \qquad O_{ij} = (P_{i+1,j} - P_{i,j}) \cdot (P_{i,j+1} - P_{ij}) ,$$

where O_{ij} corresponds to the logical "upper right" angles.

In order to control the orthogonality of the logical "lower left" angles, consider the functional O_{LL} given by

$$(4.14) \quad O_{LL} = \sum_i \sum_j \tilde{O}_{ij}^2 , \qquad \tilde{O}_{ij} = (P_{i-1,j} - P_{ij}) \cdot (P_{i,j\;1} - P_{ij}) .$$

There are similar functionals for the upper left (O_{UL}) and lower right angles (O_{LR}). The functional F_O, therefore, can be written as

$$(4.15) \qquad\qquad F_O = O_{UR} + O_{UL} + O_{LL} + O_{LR} .$$

This is a family of functionals that gives angle control; it can be opted to control the upper, lower, interior, and boundary angles. These functionals allow a great deal of flexibility, since it can be decided in advance, based on the physical region, whose angles will need more control.

4.2.6. Minimization Procedure. The minimization problem associated with the direct variational method can be solved by a nonlinear conjugate gradient method (see [7], [13], [30], and [61]) and can be posed as a least squares problem. For each functional, or for a combination of them, the number of variables becomes large very rapidly. Consequently, most standard solvers will have difficulty with these problems. In addition, any solver that stores either the full gradient or Hessian will have serious storage limitations.

It is important to note here that once the value of the length, area, or the orthogonality functional has been computed, all of the information needed to compute the gradient and the Hessian will have been obtained (see [7], [15], and [19]). Codes are under development for generating two- and three-dimensional grids that take full advantage of the theory presented in this paper. These codes have been shown to be computationally faster than other grid-generation codes [13].

4.2.7. Performance. Many examples have been generated using this code. The performance has been excellent, giving a substantial check on the method presented in this paper. In addition, the generated grids have been compared to those computed by Steinberg and Roache [67]. An appropriate combination of the two functionals' length and area produces grids suitable for numerical calculations; in addition, the orthogonality functional can be used to improve the quality of the grid angles as demonstrated by examples [14]. The capability of controlling interior and/or boundary angles gives the direct method a greater flexibility and generality.

A version of the method (length and area control only) was tested against an implementation of the homogeneous Thompson, Thames, and Mastin method [74], or Winslow method [85], which solves a coupled system of elliptic equations. The number of nonlinear iterations (iter), as well as the time in seconds, was noted for a model problem with grids of three differential sizes. Although none of the methods has been finely tuned, it seems clear that the present method is at least competitive with the most commonly used elliptic grid-generation schemes [13]. The cost of adding orthogonality control to the direct method is small; a timing test for the boundary directional angle control is given in [14].

4.3. Discrete and Continuous Length Control

Given a grid on a polygonal region Ω, we can construct a parameterization of Ω in such a way that the uniform grid of $B_2 = [0,1] \times [0,1]$ will map onto the given grid on Ω.

Let P_{ij} be the points of an $m \times n$ grid on Ω. We define the map

$$\vec{V}_{m,n} : B_2 \to \Omega$$

such that

   (1) $\vec{V}_{m,n}\left((i-1)/(m+1),(j-1)/(n+1)\right) = P_{ij}$;
   (2) $\vec{V}_{m,n}$ is extended to all B_2 by linear interpolation.

We have found in practice that the optimal grids under the functional F_S tend towards smoothness as m, n approaches infinity; i.e., the corresponding $\vec{V}_{m,n}$ tends to a smooth parameterization $\vec{V}^*$:

$$\lim_{m,n\to\infty} \vec{V}_{m,n}(\xi,\eta) = \vec{V}^*(\xi,\eta)\,.$$

In order to explain this, it will be proved that when this happens, $V^*(\xi,n)$ is the optimal continuous grid of Steinberg and Roache [67].

THEOREM 4.3.1. *Let $\bar{z}_{m,n}$ denote the optimal grid of Ω under the functional F_S, and let $\bar{V}_{m,n}(\xi,\eta)$ be the corresponding parameterization. If*

$$\lim_{m,n\to\infty} \vec{V}_{m,n}(\xi,\eta) = \vec{V}^*(\xi,\eta)$$

exists and is C^1, then

$$\lim_{m,n\to\infty} F_S(z_{m,n}) = \int \int_{B_2} \left(\left\| \frac{\partial \bar{V}^*}{\partial \xi} \right\|_2^2 + \left\| \frac{\partial \bar{V}^*}{\partial \eta} \right\|_2^2 \right) d\xi\, d\eta\,,$$

and V^* is the optimal continuous grid of Steinberg and Roache.

Proof. Let $z^*_{m,n}$ be the corresponding discrete grid to V^* on Ω, i.e.,

$$P^*_{ij} = \bar{V}^* \left(\frac{i-1}{m+1}, \frac{j-1}{n+1} \right)\,.$$

Then,

$$F_S(z_{m,n}^*) = S_H(z_{m,n}^*) + S_V(z_{m,n}^*) \ .$$

Let us consider the functional $S_H(z_{n,n}^*)$, i.e.,

$$S_H(z_{m,n}^*) = \sum_{i=1}^{m+1} \sum_{j=2}^{n+1} \ell_{ij}^2 \ ,$$

where

$$\begin{aligned}
\ell_{i,j} &= \|P_{i,j}^* - P_{i+1,j}^*\|_2^2 \\
&= \left(x^* \left(\frac{i-1}{m+1}, \frac{j-1}{n+1} \right) - x^* \left(\frac{i}{m+1}, \frac{j-1}{n+1} \right) \right)^2 \\
&\quad + \left(y^* \left(\frac{i-1}{m+1}, \frac{j-1}{n+1} \right) - y^* \left(\frac{i}{m+1}, \frac{j-1}{n+1} \right) \right)^2 ,
\end{aligned}$$

where

$$V^*(\xi, \eta) = \begin{pmatrix} x^*(\xi, \eta) \\ y^*(\xi, \eta) \end{pmatrix} \ .$$

By the Mean Value Theorem we get

$$\left[x^* \left(\frac{i-1}{m+1}, \frac{j-1}{n+1} \right) - x^* \left(\frac{i}{m+1}, \frac{j-1}{n+1} \right) \right]^2 = x_\xi^* \left(\xi_i \ , \frac{j-1}{n+1} \right)^2 \frac{1}{(m+1)^2} \ ,$$

where $(i-1)/(m+1) < \xi_i < (i)/(m+1)$. Similarly,

$$\left(y^* \left[\frac{i-1}{m+1}, \frac{j-1}{n+1} \right] - y^* \left[\frac{i}{m+1}, \frac{j-1}{n+1} \right] \right)^2 = y_\xi^* \left(\tilde{\xi}_i, \frac{j-1}{n+1} \right)^2 \frac{1}{(m+1)^2} \ ,$$

where $(i-1)/(m+1) < \tilde{\xi}_i < (i)/(m+1)$. Then,

$$\begin{aligned}
S_H(z_{m,n}^*) &= \sum_{i=1}^{m+1} \left(\sum_{j=2}^{m+1} x_\xi^* \left(\xi_i, \frac{j-1}{n+1} \right)^2 \frac{1}{m+1} \right) \frac{1}{m+1} \\
&\quad + \sum_{i=1}^{m+1} \left(\sum_{j=2}^{n+1} y_\xi^* \left(\tilde{\xi}_i, \frac{j-1}{n+1} \right)^2 \frac{1}{m+1} \right) \frac{1}{m+1}.
\end{aligned}$$

The following equation can be directly obtained:

$$\lim_{m,n \to \infty} S_H(z_{m,n}^*) = \int \int_{B_2} \left\| \frac{\partial \bar{V}^*}{\partial \xi} \right\|_2^2 d\xi \, d\eta \ .$$

In a similar way, we can get

$$\lim_{m,n \to \infty} S_V(z_{m,n}^*) = \int \int_{B_2} \left\| \frac{\partial \bar{V}^*}{\partial \eta} \right\|_2^2 d\xi \, d\eta \ ,$$

which gives us

$$\lim_{m,n\to\infty} F_S(z^*_{m,n}) = \int\int_{B_2} \left(\left\| \frac{\partial \bar{V}^*}{\partial \xi} \right\|_2^2 + \left\| \frac{\partial \bar{V}^*}{\partial \eta} \right\|_2^2 \right) d\xi\, d\eta \ .$$

If $z_{m,n}$ is the optimal grid, then

$$F_S(z_{m,n}) \le F_S(z^*_{m,n}) \ ,$$

which implies

$$\lim_{m,n\to\infty} F_S(z_{m,n}) \le \int\int_{B_2} \left(\left\| \frac{\partial V^*}{\partial \xi} \right\|_2^2 + \left\| \frac{\partial \bar{V}^*}{\partial \eta} \right\|_2^2 \right) d\xi\, d\eta \ .$$

The rest of the proof comes from the fact that if $\bar{V}^*$ were not the optimal continuous grid of Steinberg and Roache, then it would be possible to construct a discrete grid $\tilde{z}_{m,n}$, such that the value $F_S(\tilde{z}_{m,n})$ would be smaller than the corresponding $F_S(z_{m,n})$ for n sufficiently large. However, that would be a contradiction, since $z_{m,n}$ is by assumption the optimal grid.

Steinberg and Roache found that the optimal continuous grid $V^*(\xi,\eta)$ must satisfy an uncoupled system of Laplacian equations:

$$\frac{\partial^2 x^*}{\partial \xi^2} + \frac{\partial^2 x^*}{\partial \eta^2} = 0 \ ;$$

$$\frac{\partial^2 y^*}{\partial \xi^2} + \frac{\partial^2 y^*}{\partial \eta^2} = 0,$$

which agrees with the results that were obtained [7], [19]; namely, uncoupled discrete Laplacian equations.

4.4. Model Problem for Area Control

It is natural to ask, "Given Ω, is it possible to subdivide it into cells of equal area?" In this case, the points on the boundary are fixed and, as shall be seen, for some distributions of points on the boundary, this is not going to be possible.

A simple model problem is constructed that shows why there is not a general existence theorem for arbitrary distribution of the points on the boundary. Consider the unit square with $m = n = 2$, and for each fixed $0 < \alpha < 1$, consider the following distribution (see Fig. 4.1). Given α fixed, $0 < \alpha < \frac{1}{2}$, do there exist points P, Q, R, S such that all the cells of the grid have the same area? This is a quadratic problem in eight variables; some assumptions are made to simplify this problem and still produce interesting results. For $\alpha = \frac{1}{3}$ there is a trivial solution, but we do not expect to have a solution for α very small, or for α very near to .5. In order to solve this problem, we shall need the elementary result given in the following theorem.

THEOREM 4.4.1. *Given the points P_1, P_2, P_3, the set of all points P such that the quadrilateral P, P_1, P_2, P_3 has constant area c is a line parallel to $P_1 P_3$.*

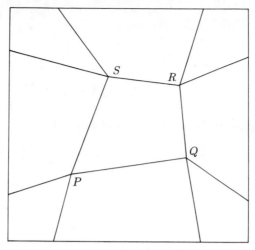

Model Problem

FIG. 4.1. *Model problems.*

Proof.

$$a(P, P_1, P_2, P_3) = \frac{1}{2}\det(P - P_2, P_1 - P_3) = c\,,$$
$$(x - x_2)(y_1 - y_3) - (y - y_2)(x_1 - x_3) = 2c\,.$$

Applying the above theorem to the corner cells shows that the points P, Q, R, S have to be on the lines (see Fig. 4.2)

$$\ell_1 : x_p + y_p = \frac{2}{9\alpha}\,,$$
$$\ell_2 : x_q - y_q = 1 - \frac{2}{9\alpha}\,,$$
$$\ell_3 : x_r + y_r = 2 - \frac{2}{9\alpha}\,,$$
$$\ell_4 : x_s - y_s = \frac{2}{9\alpha} - 1\,.$$

This reduces the problem to the four variables x_p, x_q, x_r, x_s.

Next, it is easy to check that the problem must have a solution symmetric with respect to $\left(\frac{1}{2}, \frac{1}{2}\right)$, the center of the square. For example, if

$$x_r = 1 - x_p\,,$$
$$y_r = 1 - y_p\,,$$

then

$$x_r + y_r = 2 - (x_p + y_p) = 2 - \frac{2}{9\alpha}\,.$$

This symmetry allows us to reduce the problem to two variables; we shall choose x_p, x_s.

So, now we shall solve the system

$$a(P_{12}, P, S, P_{13}) = \frac{1}{9} \, ,$$

$$a(P, Q, R, S) = \frac{1}{9} \, .$$

Straightforward simplification leads to the system

$$2\alpha x_p x_s + \left[\alpha(1 - \alpha) - \frac{2}{9} \right] (x_p + x_s) = \frac{2}{9} \, ,$$

$$\alpha x_p x_s - \frac{1}{9}(x_p + x_s) = \frac{2\alpha - 1}{9} \, .$$

Let

$$\sigma = x_p + x_s \, ,$$

$$\rho = x_p x_s \, .$$

Then we have

$$\alpha \rho + \left[\frac{\alpha(1 - \alpha)}{2} - \frac{1}{9} \right] \sigma = \frac{2}{9} \, ,$$

$$\alpha \rho - \frac{1}{9}\sigma = \frac{2\alpha - 1}{9} \, .$$

Solving for α and σ, we get

$$\sigma = \frac{2}{a\alpha} \, ,$$

$$\rho = \frac{18\alpha^2 - 9\alpha + 2}{81\alpha^2} \, .$$

From the definition of σ and ρ, we get

$$x_p^2 - \sigma x_p + \rho = 0 \, ,$$

so in order to have a solution, we need

$$\sigma^2 - 4\rho \geq 0 \, ,$$
$$18\alpha^2 - 9\alpha + 1 \leq 0 \, ,$$
$$(3\alpha - 1)(6\alpha - 1) \leq 0 \, ,$$

or

$$\frac{1}{6} \leq \alpha \leq \frac{1}{3} \, .$$

Consequently, the following theorem has been proved.

THEOREM 4.4.2. *For the model problem, there are equal area solutions only for* $\frac{1}{6} \leq \alpha \leq \frac{1}{3}$ *and*

$$x_p(\alpha) = \begin{cases} \frac{1 - \sqrt{(1 - 3\alpha)(6\alpha - 1)}}{9\alpha} \\ \frac{1 + \sqrt{(1 - 3\alpha)(6\alpha - 1)}}{9\alpha} \end{cases} \, , \qquad \frac{1}{6} < \alpha < \frac{1}{3} \, .$$

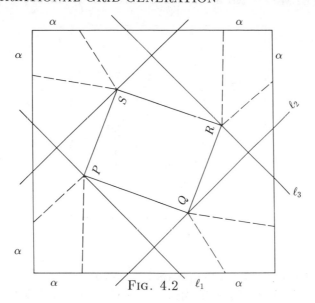

FIG. 4.2

4.4.1. Critical Points. Where are the critical points of F_A when

$$\alpha \notin \left[\frac{1}{6}, \frac{1}{3}\right]?$$

The following theorem gives a clue to the answer.

THEOREM 4.4.3. *Assume that we are given P, Q, R, S. Then:*

(i) *If P', Q', R', S' are the corresponding symmetrical points of P, Q, R, S with respect to $y = \frac{1}{2}$, then*

$$F_A(P, S, Q, R) = F_A(S', P', R', Q') .$$

(ii) *If P'', Q'', R'', S'' are the corresponding symmetrical points P, Q, R, S with respect to $x = \frac{1}{2}$, then*

$$F_A(P, S, Q, R) = F_A(Q'', R'', P'', S'') .$$

Proof. Observe Fig. 4.3 below. Let A'_{ij} denote the value of the areas of the cells when we take the ordered points S', R', Q', P'. From the symmetry of the square it is easy to obtain that

$$A'_{11} = A_{13} , \qquad A'_{21} = A_{23} , \qquad A'_{31} = A_{33} ,$$
$$A'_{13} = A_{11} , \qquad A'_{23} = A_{21} , \qquad A'_{33} = A_{31} ,$$

and also that

$$A'_{21} = A_{21} , \qquad A'_{22} = A_{22} , \qquad A'_{23} = A_{23} .$$

Therefore,

$$F_A(P, S, W, R) = F_A(S', P', R', Q') .$$

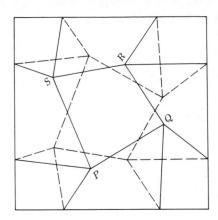

FIG. 4.3

The proof of the second affirmation is similar.

It is expected that F_A will have a critical point when P and S are symmetrical with respect to $y = \frac{1}{2}$, P and Q are symmetrical with respect to $x = \frac{1}{2}$, and S and R are symmetrical with respect to $x = \frac{1}{2}$. If such a critical point exists, then the following theorem shows how to compute it.

THEOREM 4.4.4. *If $P^t = (x_p, y_p)$, $S^t = (x_p, 1 - y_p)$, $Q^t = (1 - x_p, y_p)$, and $P^t = (1 - x_p, 1 - y_p)$, then F_A has at least one critical point on this set of grids, and at the critical points we have that $x_p = y_p$.*

Proof. From the definition it is easy to check that (see Fig. 4.4)

$$A_{11} = A_{13} = A_{31} = A_{33},$$

$$A_{12} = A_{32}, \qquad A_{21} = A_{23};$$

then

$$F_A = 4A_{11}^2 + 2A_{12}^2 + 2A_{21}^2 + A_{22}^2.$$

Straightforward computation gives us

$$A_{11} = \frac{\alpha(x_p + y_p)}{2},$$
$$A_{12} = x_p(1 - \alpha - y_p),$$
$$A_{21} = y_p(1 - \alpha - x_p),$$
$$A_{22} = (2x_p - 1)(1y_p - 1);$$

then

$$F_A = \alpha^2(x_p + y_p)^2 + 2x_p^2(1 - \alpha - y_p)^2 + 2y_p^2(1 - \alpha - x_p)^2 + (2x_p - 1)^2(2y_p - 1)^2.$$

Note that F_A is symmetric with respect to x_p and y_p.

Let us consider the case when $x_p = y_p$. Let $f(x_p, \alpha)$ denote the value of F_A in this case; then we have

$$f(x_p, \alpha) = 4\alpha^2 x_p^2 + 4x_p^2(1 - \alpha - x_p)^2 + (2x_p - 1)^4$$
$$= 20x_p^4 + (8\alpha - 40)x_p^3 + (8\alpha^2 - 8\alpha + 28)x_p^2 - 8x_p + 1.$$

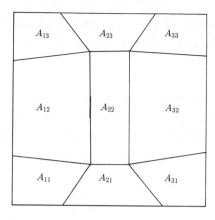

FIG. 4.4

The derivative of $f(x_p, \alpha)$ with respect to x_p is a cubic polynomial in x_p given by

$$f'(x_p, \alpha) = 80x_p^3 + (24\alpha - 120)x_p^2 + (16\alpha^2 - 16\alpha + 56)x_p - 8 \ .$$

Thus, $f'(x_p, \alpha)$ has at least one real root, so this concludes the proof of the theorem. $\square$

Note that the values of α for which we have three real roots can be computed; from the discriminant of the cubic, a six-degree polynomial will result:

$$284a^6 - 528a^5 + 2412a^4 - 1136a^3 + 99a^2 + 30a - 5,$$

which has only two real roots, one negative and the other positive. This last root is of interest for the model problem and is equal to

$$\alpha = .2591 \cdots ,$$

so that for $\alpha < .2591$ we have three real solutions of $f'(x_p, \alpha)$ that are saddle points of F_A. In order to do a complete analysis of this problem, the symbol manipulation program MACSYMA will be used to do the required algebra. However, the FORTRAN code described in §4.3 is used to calculate the critical points for this model problem. This is done by choosing a large variety of initial guesses for the grid and then letting the code find a critical point; no points other than those predicted by the above calculations were ever found.

These results are illustrated in Figs. 4.5–4.14, which are presented at the end of this section. The figures all show a 4-by-4 grid for the model problem discussed at the beginning of this section. The figures present the grids that correspond to all of the critical points of the area control problem for a progression of values of α; some critical points are minima and others are saddle points. The drawings were made using the code described in §4.3.

It is easy to check that for a 3-by-3 grid the area functional is only quadratic. In the 4-by-4 case, the functional is quartic. However, the number of unknowns is smaller than the number of areas, so the corresponding least squares problem has complete rank. In the 5-by-5 case the number of unknowns is greater than the number of areas, so this problem has incomplete rank. Again, we hope to use MACSYMA to analyze this problem.

4.5. Conclusions

The direct variational grid-generation method presented here is a robust and efficient method for grid generation. As shown in [13], area control by itself is not adequate, but a proper combination of area and length control has the capability of generating grids suitable for numerical calculations. The capability of these methods is greatly enhanced by the orthogonality functional. Moreover, it is clear that the method has a natural, but not straightforward, extension to three dimensions; these problems will have a structure analogous to the two-dimensional problem. Thus, it is reasonable to expect that the three-dimensional method will also be competitive with other standard grid-generation methods. Furthermore, the discrete length functional converges to the continuous length and the model problem for the area functional shows how the distribution of the points on the boundary affects the the existence of equal area solutions.

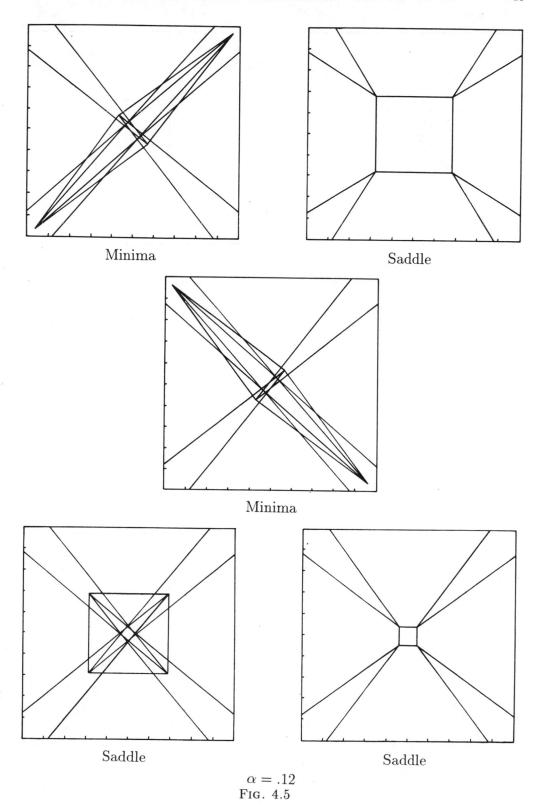

$\alpha = .12$

FIG. 4.5

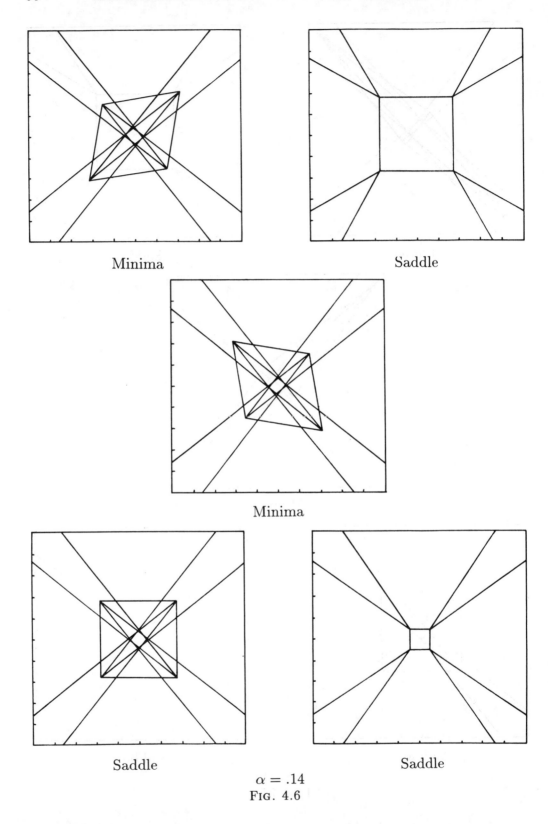

Minima

Saddle

Minima

Saddle

Saddle

$\alpha = .14$

FIG. 4.6

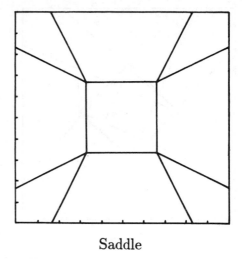

Saddle

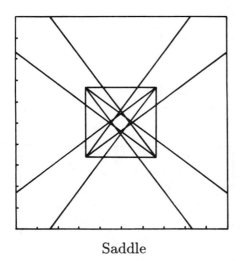

Saddle   Saddle

$$\alpha = 1/6$$

Fig. 4.7

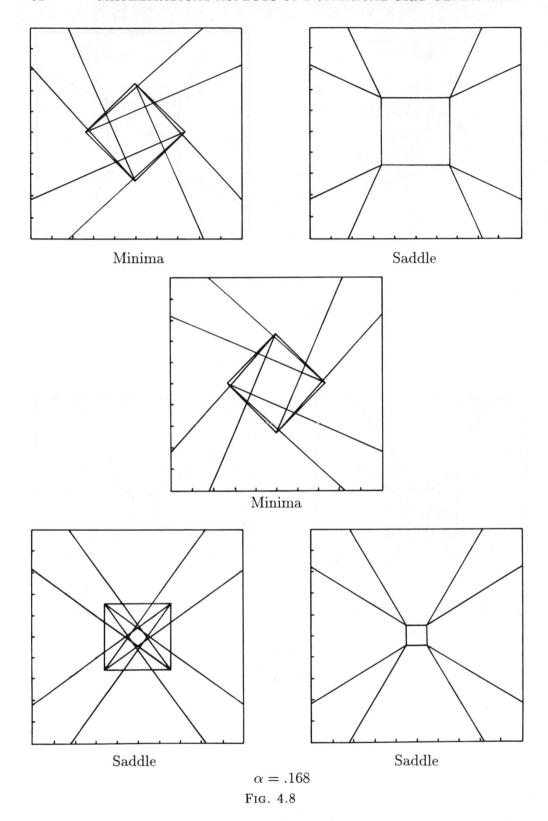

$\alpha = .168$

Fig. 4.8

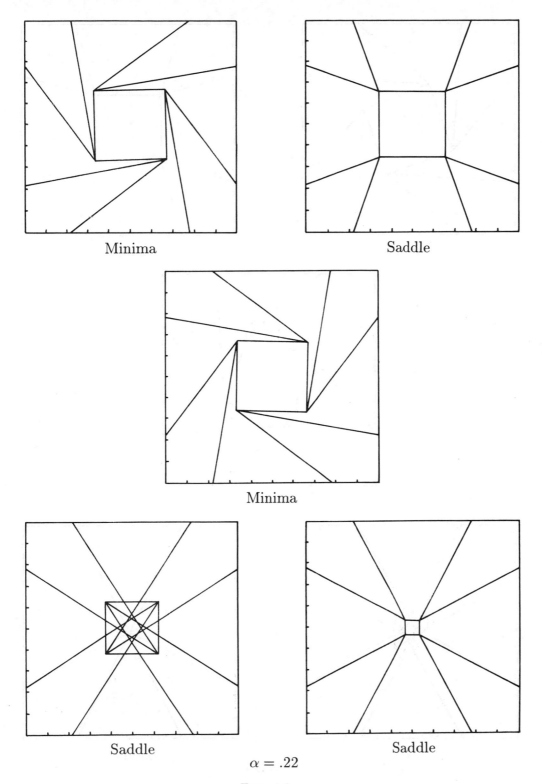

Minima

Saddle

Minima

Saddle

Saddle

$\alpha = .22$

FIG. 4.9

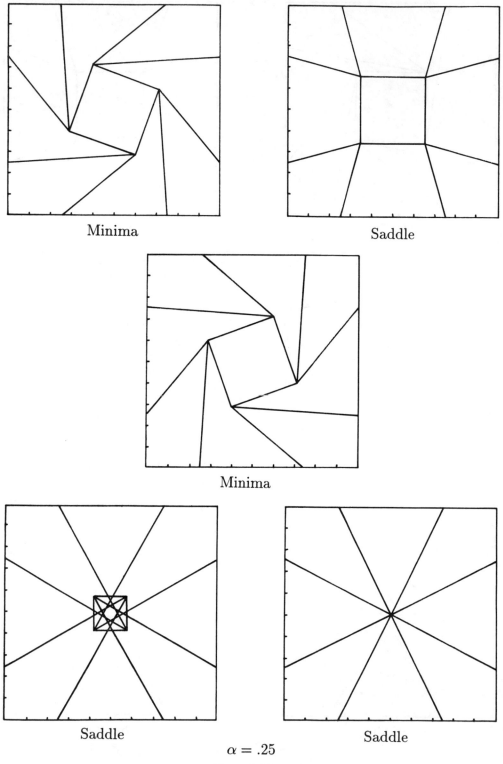

Minima

Saddle

Minima

Saddle

Saddle

$\alpha = .25$

FIG. 4.10

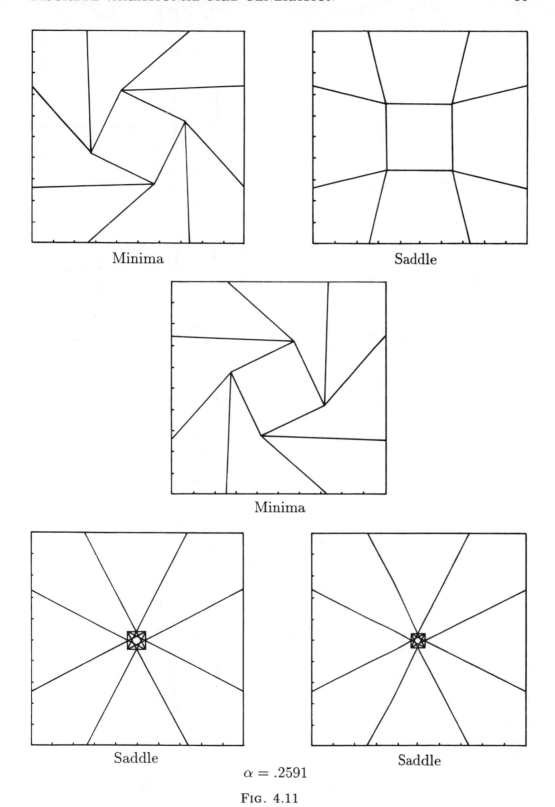

Minima

Saddle

Minima

Saddle

Saddle

$\alpha = .2591$

Fig. 4.11

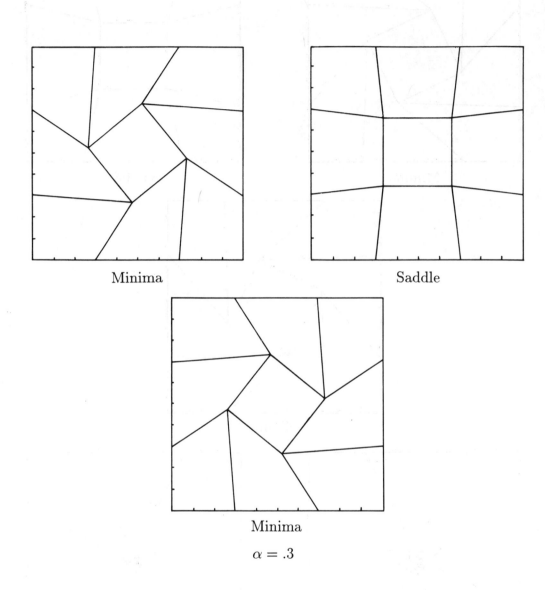

Minima

Saddle

Minima

$\alpha = .3$

FIG. 4.12

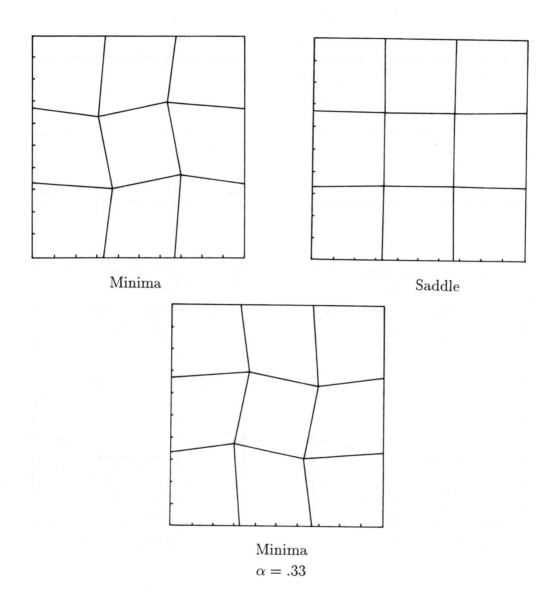

Minima

Saddle

Minima
$\alpha = .33$

FIG. 4.13

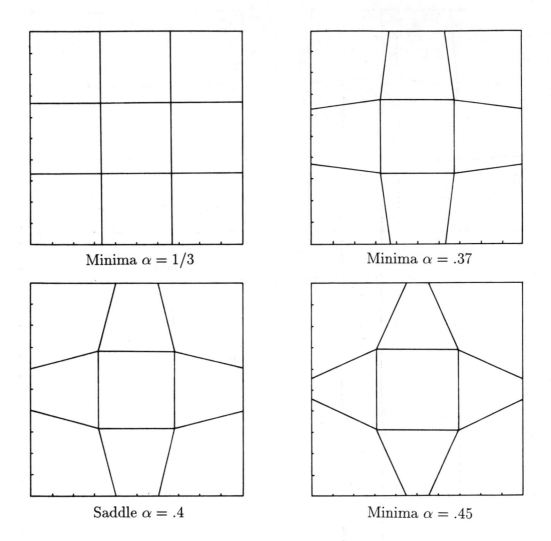

Minima $\alpha = 1/3$ Minima $\alpha = .37$

Saddle $\alpha = .4$ Minima $\alpha = .45$

Fig. 4.14

Chapter 5

Bifurcation of Grids on Curves

S. Steinberg and P. J. Roache

5.1. Background

Attempts to use variational grid-generation methods to generate grids on certain surfaces of modest shape have failed to produce suitable grids. There were sufficient points in the grids to well-resolve the surface, so the failures were not easily explained. Similar difficulties were found for the analogous problem of variational grid generation on curves; those problems are caused by multiple solutions of the underlying nonlinear algebraic equations, as shown in this paper. Thus the difficulty is intrinsic to the discrete approximation of the variational problem used to generate the grids. For a description of the variational techniques, more details concerning the anomalous behavior of the grid-generation algorithm for both curves and surfaces, and a discussion of how symmetry of the difference equations affects the grid generator, see papers [65], [66], and [67], by Steinberg and Roache. A significantly improved surface grid generator is currently being developed by Knupp [43].

The difficulties with the grid generator are best described in terms of bifurcations, thus, we choose a family of curves that depend on a parameter. Throughout this paper we use the family of simple parabolas

$$(5.1) \qquad y = \alpha\,x\,(1-x), \qquad 0 \le x \le 1, \qquad \alpha \ge 0,$$

all of which depend on the parameter α. For $\alpha = 0$ the curve is a straight line that is trivial to grid; as α grows, the curvature increases and the curve becomes more difficult to grid. Several other curves were tested with similar results.

The grid-generation algorithm is obtained by calculating the Euler–Lagrange equation for a variational problem and then discretizing this equation using centered differences. In the case of curves, the solution of the Euler–Lagrange equation is simply the arclength parameterization. Thus, the continuum problems possess a unique solution, which means that the bifurcation diagram for this problem is trivial, as shown in §5.2. Next, it is shown that the variational problem has a positive Hessian that is not bounded below. The lack of a lower bound is an indicator that there will be difficulties in the discrete problems. In addition, two iterative methods for calculating the solution of the grid-generation equation are presented. The *fully lagged* iteration has rather poor convergence properties, whereas the *nominal* iteration has problems only at bifurcation points.

In §5.3, the most trivial discrete grid-generation problem possible is analyzed. In such problems, the grids have one free point and two fixed boundary points. Here, the bifurcation diagram is decidedly nontrivial in all the examples studied; the grid undergoes a pitchfork bifurcation as the parameter increases.

In §5.4, the results of some numerical experiments for the nominal iteration are presented. First, the bifurcation of the grid with one free point is confirmed. Experiments with grids that have a reasonable number of points show that the grids bifurcate. However, the multiple solutions disappear when the resolution is sufficiently high. Note that the behavior of the solution of discrete problems with a reasonable number of points is more like the problem with one free point than the continuum problem.

Bifurcation studies have been carried out for the problem

$$(5.2) \qquad x''(t) + \lambda\, f(x(t)) = 0\,, \qquad x(0) = 0\,, \qquad x(1) = 1\,,$$

where λ is the bifurcation parameter (see Bigge and Bohl [8]; Peitgen, Saupe, and Schmitt [53]; and Stuart [69]). The results for this problem are strikingly similar to the results obtained in this paper. On the other hand, the grid-generation equations are not covered by the results of these papers.

There is reason to believe that the difficulties encountered in curve grid generation will show up in other grid-generation problems. First, there are the results of the above-mentioned bifurcation studies. Second, when the Euler–Lagrange equation for a variational problem is used to generate the grid on a curve, a quasi-linear boundary-value problem of the form

$$(5.3) \qquad x''(t) + g(x(t))\,(x'(t))^2 = 0\,, \qquad x(0) = 0\,, \qquad x(1) = 1$$

must be solved. Many of the differential equations used to generate one-dimensional grids have this form, where

$$(5.4) \qquad g(x) = (\ln(f(x)))' = \frac{f'(x)}{f(x)}\,.$$

Some examples are given in [4, Eq. 3] and (5.17). When comparing (5.2) to equations used by others, it is helpful to note that

$$(5.5) \qquad \frac{d}{d\xi}g(x) = g'(x)\, x'\,.$$

The equation for defining a grid equidistributed with respect to a position-dependent weight $w(x)$ (i.e., solution-adaptive grid) is given by

$$(5.6) \qquad x'(\xi)\, w(x(\xi)) = C$$

(see [75, p. 371, Eq. (4)]). The derivative of this equation with respect to t gives a second-order differential equation for $x(\xi)$, which is the same as the equation for the variational problem defining the adaptive grid (see [67]):

$$(5.7) \qquad x''(\xi) + \frac{w'(x(\xi))}{w(x(\xi))}(x'(\xi))^2 = 0 \,.$$

Since w in (5.7) plays a role identical to that of f in (5.4), it is clearly possible for the anomalies that cause difficulties in curve grid generation to appear in solution-adaptive grid-generation problems.

The results in this paper make it clear that the anomalies occur because the discrete grid-generation problem has many solutions. In the one-free-point problem, the grid undergoes a pitchfork bifurcation as the parameter α increases. For grids with a modest number of points on moderate curves, the numerical method finds a multitude of stable solutions while the desired solution is unstable, and thus, not computable. This is illustrated in Fig. 5.1, where several anomalous grids, computed using the algorithm described below, are shown.

In this figure, the curves are the parabolas described above. All grids contain nine points, including the boundary points. The first curve illustrates a typical random grid that was used for the initial condition. The grid on the curve of height one-half is not anomalous and is, in fact, an excellent result. If the curve is of height one or higher, then the nominal iteration bifurcates and there are multiple solutions; this is illustrated by the remaining curves. With sufficiently high resolution for a given curve, the method finds a unique appropriate solution; however, these grids contain substantially more points than are necessary to resolve the curve.

The analysis given here provides substantial insight into the difficulties of generating grids on curves and surfaces. More recent results of Knupp [43] indicate that there are algorithms that do not have bifurcation problems. However, the algorithms are not a simple modification of the existing variational methods.

Many of the algebraic calculations in this paper are done or checked by using the symbol manipulator MACSYMA [78]. Also, the results in §5.2 can be made rigorous by formulating them in a Hilbert or Banach space setting. The rigorous results provide no additional insight, so they were not pursued.

5.2. Continuum Case

A continuum grid is merely a reparameterization of a curve. Thus, the problem is, essentially, to reparameterize a curve using arclength. Such problems have been studied by a number of authors (see Steinberg and Roache [67]; or Thompson, Warsi, and Mastin [75]). The questions of the existence and uniqueness of the grid are settled by giving explicit expression for the reparameterization. The related variational problem is shown to have a positive Hessian, which is not bounded below. Two iterative methods for finding the

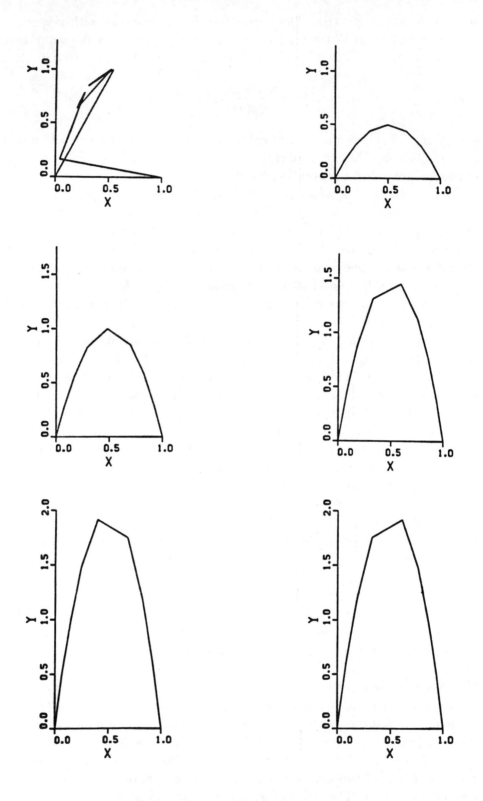

FIG. 5.1. *Anomalous grids.*

solution of the Euler–Lagrange equation, the fully lagged and the nominal, are analyzed. The nominal iteration is decidedly superior.

5.2.1. Curves. The arclength and its differential frequently appear in these calculations (surprisingly, the curvature does not play a direct role [65]). Let a curve (in vector form) be given by

$$(5.8) \qquad R(r) = (x(r), y(r), z(r))$$

and its derivative be given by

$$(5.9) \qquad R'(r) = (x'(r), y'(r), z'(r)).$$

Then, the r derivative of the arclength s is given by

$$(5.10) \qquad \frac{ds}{dr} = \|R'(r)\| = \sqrt{(x'(r))^2 + (y'(r))^2 + (z'(r))^2} = L(r),$$

and the length of a segment of the curve between $r = 0$ and r is given by

$$(5.11) \qquad s = s(r) = \int_0^r L(\rho)\, d\rho.$$

It is always assumed that
$$(5.12) \qquad L(r) > 0,$$

which implies that the arclength is always a strictly increasing function of r. For convenience, define
$$(5.13) \qquad S(r) = L^2(r),$$

and then note that
$$(5.14) \qquad \frac{d}{dr} \ln S(r) = \frac{S'(r)}{S(r)} = 2\frac{L'(r)}{L(r)}.$$

5.2.2. Equidistributed Grids on Curves. Equidistribution of points on a curve requires that the arclengths between gridpoints should be equal. The developments in Steinberg and Roache [66], [67] discuss how to use a variational technique to generate a continuum grid on a curve, so that the grid is distributed according to some given weight. The variational problem for equidistributing the grid is to minimize

$$(5.15) \qquad I(r) = \int_0^1 (L(r)\, r')^2\, d\xi = \int_0^1 S(r)\, (r')^2\, d\xi$$

over all functions $r = r(\xi)$ with $r(0) = 0$ and $r(1) = 1$. The Euler–Lagrange equation for the minimization problem is

$$(5.16) \qquad 2\, S(r)\, r'' + S'(r)\, (r')^2 = 0, \qquad r(0) = 0, \qquad r(1) = 1.$$

Recall that $S(r) = L^2(r)$, so, in terms of the differential of arclength, the previous equation becomes

$$(5.17) \qquad r'' + \frac{L'(r)}{L(r)}(r')^2 = 0, \qquad r(0) = 0, \qquad r(1) = 1.$$

This boundary-value problem always possesses a unique solution $r = r(\xi)$ and the inverse of this solution, $\xi = \xi(r)$, is a normalized arclength, as the following discussion shows.

First, note that $r = $ constant is a solution of the differential equation (with $r'(\xi) \equiv 0$). To find another solution, assume that r' is not identically zero. Then, one integration of (5.16) gives

$$(5.18) \qquad S(r)(r')^2 = K^2,$$

where $K > 0$ because the left-hand side of (5.18) is greater than or equal to zero, and not identically zero. Also, because $S(r) > 0$ and $K > 0$, $r'(\xi) \neq 0$. This equation cannot, in general, be solved for r as an explicit function of ξ. However, the equation can be rewritten as

$$(5.19) \qquad \frac{d\xi}{dr} = \frac{1}{r'} = \frac{\sqrt{S(r)}}{K} = \frac{L(r)}{K}.$$

Another integration and the boundary conditions give

$$(5.20) \qquad \xi = \frac{\int_0^r L(\tau)\, d\tau}{\int_0^1 L(\tau)\, d\tau}.$$

This implies that ξ is a normalized arclength, $s = K\xi$. Note that (5.19) implies that $d\xi/dr > 0$, so the previous equation can always be inverted for $r = r(\xi)$. The inverse function is clearly a nonconstant solution of (5.16). Thus, the continuum grid is given by a normalized arclength; this is exactly what is meant by an equidistributed grid.

5.2.3. The Hessian.   The functional $I(r)$ given in the previous section has a minimum at a point $\tilde{r}$ in the space of smooth functions if, for each direction a at the point $\tilde{r}$, the first derivative of the functional is zero and the second derivative is positive. More precisely, let $a = a(\xi)$ and $b = b(\xi)$ be smooth with support in the interior of $[0,1]$. The directional derivative (in the direction a at $\tilde{r}$) is given by

$$(5.21) \qquad D_a I(\tilde{r}) = \frac{d}{d\varepsilon} I(\tilde{r} + \varepsilon\, a)\Big|_{\varepsilon=0},$$

while the mixed second derivative is given by

$$(5.22) \qquad D_b D_a I(\tilde{r}) = \frac{d}{d\varepsilon} D_a I(\tilde{r} + \varepsilon\, b)\Big|_{\varepsilon=0}.$$

The functional has a minimum at $\tilde{r}$, provided that

(5.23)
$$D_a I(\tilde{r}) \equiv 0, \qquad D_a^2 I(\tilde{r}) > 0,$$

for all $a \neq 0$ satisfying the conditions given above.

The computation of $D_a I$ and $D_a^2 I$ is a straightforward application of differentiation and integration by parts

(5.24)
$$D_a I(r) = -\int_0^1 \left(2\,S(r)\,r'' + S'(r)\,(r')^2\right) a \, d\xi,$$

(5.25)
$$D_a^2 I(r) = \int_0^1 \left(2\,S(r)\,(a')^2 + 4\,S'(r)\,r'\,a\,a' + S''(r)\,(r')^2\,a^2\right) d\xi.$$

The requirement that $D_a I(\tilde{r}) \equiv 0$ for all a implies that

(5.26)
$$2\,S(\tilde{r})\,\tilde{r}'' + S'(\tilde{r})\,(\tilde{r}')^2 = 0,$$

which is nothing but the Euler–Lagrange equation (5.16) for the minimization of $I(r)$. The discussions in previous sections show that the functional has a unique critical point, which is given by the arclength parameterization of the curve. However, this critical point is not necessarily a minimum. Even though, in general, there is no simple formula for the critical point of the minimization problem (i.e., the solution of the Euler–Lagrange equation), this critical point is, in fact, always a minimum. To show this, integrate (5.26) (i.e., eq. (5.18)), and then use differentiation and the chain rule to obtain

(5.27)
$$S(\tilde{r}) = \frac{K^2}{(\tilde{r}')^2}, \qquad S'(\tilde{r}) = \frac{-2\,K^2}{(\tilde{r}')^4}, \qquad S''(\tilde{r}) = \frac{8\,K^2}{(\tilde{r}')^6},$$

where $K > 0$ and $r'(\xi) > 0$. Substituting this into the second derivative of the functional gives

(5.28)
$$D_a^2 I(\tilde{r}) = 2K^2 \int_0^1 \frac{(a'\,\tilde{r}' - 2\,a)^2}{(\tilde{r}')^4}\, d\xi.$$

This expression is always greater than or equal to zero, and can equal zero only if the factor in the numerator is zero. Given $\tilde{r}$, an a that makes the numerator identically zero can always be computed. However, the ordinary differential equation (ODE) satisfied by a implies that if $a(\xi)$ is zero at one point, then $a \equiv 0$. Because a has zero boundary conditions, the second derivative of the functional is always positive in every allowable direction, and thus, the normalized arclength parameterization is a minimum. On the other hand, if a is the solution of the ODE except near the boundary points, where a is made to go smoothly to zero, the integral in (5.28) can be made arbitrarily small, and consequently, the second derivative cannot be uniformly bounded below. This indicates the possibility of serious computational problems.

Example. The family of parabolas given in (5.1) and parameterized by α is used as an example throughout this paper. The parameter α is used to adjust the height $(= \alpha/4)$ of the curve. To apply the above results, write the curve (5.1) in parametric form:

$$(5.29) \qquad x = r, \qquad y = \alpha r(1 - r), \qquad z = 0, \qquad 0 \leq r \leq 1.$$

The Euler–Lagrange equation for this problem can be integrated (as noted above). However, this gives an implicit solution for r as a function of ξ (in fact, an explicit solution for ξ as a function of r) that is transcendental and not explicitly solvable for r as a function of ξ (the solution $\xi(r)$ can easily be computed using MACSYMA). In any case, this solution is a minimum of the functional for any value of α. This is in sharp contrast with what is found for discrete approximations of the Euler–Lagrange equation.

5.2.4. The Fully Lagged Iteration. The fully lagged iteration has the worst convergence properties of the algorithms studied. However, in multidimensional problems, the analogues of this algorithm require minimal storage, therefore, such algorithms are advantageous when this is a consideration. This iteration is written in the form of an integrodifferential equation, so that its convergence properties are clear.

The fully lagged iteration is based on writing the differential equation so that the linearized version is as simple as possible (i.e., as much of the differential equation as possible is written on the right-hand side of the equation; putting things on the right-hand side of the equation is referred to as lagging). The fully lagged form of the boundary-value problem is

$$(5.30) \qquad r''(\xi) = -\frac{S'(r(\xi))}{2S(r(\xi))}(r'(\xi))^2, \qquad r(0) = 0, \qquad r(1) = 1,$$

where $r = r(\xi)$ is to be found and $S(r)$ is a given function. The fully lagged iteration is

$$(5.31) \quad r''_{n+1}(\xi) = -\frac{S'(r_n(\xi))}{2S(r_n(\xi))}(r'_n(\xi))^2, \qquad r_{n+1}(0) = 0, \qquad r_{n+1}(1) = 1,$$

for $n \geq 0$. A typical initial guess is $r_0(\xi) = \xi$.

The Green's function for the second derivative with the given boundary conditions is

$$(5.32) \qquad G(\xi, \tau) = \tau(\xi - 1)H(\xi - \tau) + \xi(\tau - 1)H(\tau - \xi),$$

where H is the usual Heaviside function. If

$$(5.33) \qquad F(r)(\xi) = -\int_0^1 G(\xi, \tau)\frac{S'(r(\tau))}{2S(r(\tau))}(r'(\tau))^2\, d\tau,$$

then (5.31) is equivalent to

$$(5.34) \qquad r_{n+1} = F(r_n), \qquad n \geq 0,$$

with r_0 given. Note that it is easy to formulate this operator in a Banach space setting where F is compact (and nonlinear).

Convergence of the iteration depends on the directional derivative of F at r in the direction c, which was defined as

$$(5.35) \qquad D_c F(r) = \frac{d}{d\varepsilon} F(r + \varepsilon\, c)\Big|_{\varepsilon=0}.$$

Here $c = c(\xi)$, with $c(0) = c(1) = 0$. If $\tilde{r} = F(\tilde{r})$ and $\|D_c F(\tilde{r})\| < \|c\|$, for all c and some appropriate norm, then the Picard iteration converges to $\tilde{r}$. A short computation gives

$$
\begin{aligned}
(5.36) \qquad D_c F(\tilde{r})(\xi) = {} & \int_0^1 G(\xi,\tau) \frac{(r'(\tau))^2\, S''(r(\tau))}{2\, S(r(\tau))} c(\tau)\, d\tau \\
& - \int_0^1 G(\xi,\tau) \left(\frac{r'(\tau)\, S'(r(\tau))}{S(r(\tau))} \right)^2 c(\tau)\, d\tau \\
& + \int_0^1 G_\tau(\xi,\tau) \frac{r'(\tau)\, S'(r(\tau))}{S(r(\tau))} c(\tau)\, d\tau.
\end{aligned}
$$

The critical quantities in $D_c F$ are:

$$(5.37) \qquad C_1 = \frac{S'(r)}{S(r)}, \qquad C_2 = \frac{S''(r)}{2\, S(r)} - \left(\frac{S'(r)}{S(r)} \right)^2.$$

The norm of $D_c F$ depends on S' and S'', and both involve the first, second, and third derivatives of the coordinates of the curve. The curvature of the curve depends only on the first and second derivatives of the coordinates, so convergence of the iteration depends on more than the curvature.

Example. For the parabolas given in (5.29), the expressions for the second critical quantity is complicated; neither the first nor second expression for the critical quantity is illuminating. However, the limits of these expressions for α large show that there are problems:

$$(5.38) \qquad \lim_{\alpha \to \infty} C_1 = \frac{4}{2\,r - 1}, \qquad \lim_{\alpha \to \infty} C_2 = -\frac{12}{(2\,r - 1)^2}.$$

Note that all limits are infinite for $r = \frac{1}{2}$, so convergence problems are expected for large α.

5.2.5. The Nominal Iteration.
The nominal iteration keeps as much information as possible in the linearized equation. The boundary-value problem is written

$$(5.39) \qquad r'' + \frac{S'(r)}{2\, S(r)} (r')^2 = 0, \qquad r(0) = 0, \qquad r(1) = 1;$$

and the iteration scheme is

(5.40) $r''_{n+1} + \left(\dfrac{S'(r_n)}{2\,S(r_n)} r'_n \right) r'_{n+1} = 0 \,, \qquad r_{n+1}(0) = 0 \,, \qquad r_{n+1}(1) = 1 \,.$

Set

(5.41) $$g(r) = \dfrac{S'(r)}{2\,S(r)} r' \,,$$

so that the iteration becomes

(5.42) $r''_{n+1} + g(r_n)\, r'_{n+1} = 0 \,, \qquad r_{n+1}(0) = 0 \,, \qquad r_{n+1}(1) = 1 \,.$

Note that

(5.43) $$g(r) = \dfrac{1}{2} \dfrac{d}{d\xi} (\ln S(r)) \,.$$

The equation for this iteration can be integrated. Rewrite the iteration as

(5.44) $$\dfrac{r''_{n+1}}{r'_{n+1}} + g(r_n) = 0 \,,$$

and integrate with respect to ξ to obtain

(5.45) $$\ln(r'_{n+1}) + \dfrac{1}{2} \ln(S(r_n)) = C \,.$$

This implies that $r'_{n+1} L(r_n) = C$, or

(5.46) $$r_{n+1}(\xi) = \int_0^\xi \dfrac{C}{L(r_n(\tau))}\, d\tau \,,$$

where

(5.47) $$\dfrac{1}{C} = \int_0^1 \dfrac{1}{L(r_n(\tau))}\, d\tau \,.$$

Thus, the iteration can be written as

(5.48) $$r_{n+1} = F(r_n) \,, \qquad F(r) = \dfrac{\int_0^\xi (d\tau / L(r(\tau)))}{\int_0^1 (d\tau / L(r(\tau)))} \,.$$

The directional derivative $D_c F(r)$ of this functional involves only one nontrivial term:

(5.49) $$\int_0^\xi \dfrac{S'(r(\tau))\, c(\tau)}{S^{3/2}(r(\tau))}\, d\tau \,.$$

Therefore, the critical quantity to estimate, in order to show convergence of this iteration, is $C_f = S'(r)/S^{3/2}(r)$. The square of this quantity is one of the terms in the curvature, but otherwise it is not closely related to it.

   Example. For the parabolas given in (5.29), C_f is complicated; however, C_f is small for α small or large. The numerical algorithm that implements the nominal iteration does converge well for large values of the parameters; however, there is an additional problem, which is explained below.

5.3. One-Point Grids

In this section, grids that contain one free point and two fixed-boundary points are analyzed and used to illustrate various ideas discussed in §5.2. One-point grids make a good starting point for the numerical experiments that are described in the next section. In fact, the one-point grid is a far better model than the continuum, even when computing grids that well-resolve the curve.

5.3.1. Multiple Solutions.

The grid is calculated by solving a discretized version of the Euler–Lagrange equation,

$$(5.50) \qquad 2\, S(r)\, r'' + S'(r)\,(r')^2 = 0\,, \qquad r(0) = 0\,, \qquad r(1) = 1\,,$$

for $r = r(\xi)$, $0 \le \xi \le 1$. This equation is discretized using centered differences. The one-free-point grid is given by $\xi = 0$, $\xi = \frac{1}{2}$, and $\xi = 1$; corresponding $r = r(\xi)$ values are $r = 0$, $r = r(\frac{1}{2})$, and $r = 1$. Consequently,

$$(5.51) \qquad r' \cong \frac{1-0}{1} = 1\,, \qquad r'' \cong \frac{1 - 2\,r + 0}{\frac{1}{2}^2} = 4\,(1 - 2\,r)\,.$$

The discretized Euler–Lagrange equation for the one free point is then

$$(5.52) \qquad 8\,(1 - 2\,r)\,S(r) + S'(r) = 0\,.$$

This is typically a transcendental algebraic equation for the value of r. As this equation typically is nonlinear, it can easily have multiple solutions. This equation can be integrated as follows:

$$(5.53) \qquad S(r) = e^{8(r^2 - r - A)}\,, \qquad S(0) = e^{-8A}\,.$$

Now A can be determined from the parameterization of the curve and, again, (5.53) is a transcendental algebraic equation for r.

The numerical algorithms attempt to find a solution of (5.52). The numerical grid-generation codes will have difficulties if this equation has multiple solutions.

Example. For the family of parabolas given in (5.29), the problem is to choose a point r that divides this curve into two pieces of equal length (clearly, the solution should be $r = \frac{1}{2}$). From (5.13)

$$(5.54) \qquad S(r) = 1 + \alpha^2\,(1 - 2\,r)^2\,, \qquad S'(r) = -4\,\alpha^2\,(1 - 2\,r)\,,$$

and thus

$$(5.55) \qquad \frac{S'(r)}{S(r)} = -\frac{4\,(1 - 2\,r)}{1/\alpha^2 + (1 - 2\,r)^2}\,.$$

The discretized Euler–Lagrange equation is

$$(5.56) \qquad 8\,(1 - 2\,r) = \frac{4\,(1 - 2\,r)}{1/\alpha^2 + (1 - 2\,r)^2}\,.$$

As desired, $r = \frac{1}{2}$ is a solution of this equation. If $r \neq \frac{1}{2}$, then the equation becomes

(5.57)
$$(1 - 2\,r)^2 = \frac{1}{2} - \frac{1}{\alpha^2}\,.$$

If $\alpha^2 < 2$, this equation has no real solutions; if $\alpha^2 = 2$, then $r = \frac{1}{2}$ is a double root; if $\alpha^2 > 2$, then

(5.58)
$$r_\pm = \frac{1}{2} \pm \frac{1}{2}\sqrt{\frac{1}{2} - \frac{1}{\alpha^2}}$$

are two real roots of the equation. For α large, these roots are approximately

(5.59)
$$r_\pm = \frac{1}{2} \pm \frac{\sqrt{2}}{4}\,.$$

This example shows that the intuitive argument given in Steinberg and Roache [67] about dividing curves into pieces of equal arclength does not apply to all solutions of the discretized Euler–Lagrange equation.

5.3.2. Iteration.   Both the fully lagged iteration and the nominal iteration for a one-point grid are the same because the expression for r' (using centered differences) does not involve the unknown point. Recall that the fully lagged iteration is based on solving the differential equation for the second derivative:

(5.60)
$$r'' = -\frac{S'(r)}{S(r)}(r')^2\,, \qquad r(0) = 0\,, \qquad r(1) = 1\,.$$

For one free point, the discretized equation is

(5.61)
$$4\,(1 - 2\,r) = -\frac{S'(r)}{2\,S(r)}\,.$$

The iteration is given by

(5.62)
$$4\,(1 - 2\,r_{k+1}) = -\frac{S'(r_k)}{2\,S(r_k)}\,,$$

or

(5.63)
$$r_{k+1} = g(r_k)\,, \qquad g(r) = \frac{1}{2}\left(1 + \frac{S'(r)}{8\,S(r)}\right)\,.$$

If $\tilde{r}$ is a fixed point, $\tilde{r} = g(\tilde{r})$, then the iteration converges if $|g'(\tilde{r})| < 1$. Now,

(5.64)
$$g'(r) = \frac{1}{16}\left\{\frac{S''(r)}{S(r)} - \left(\frac{S'(r)}{S(r)}\right)^2\right\}\,.$$

Example. For the parabolas given in (5.29),

(5.65)
$$g'\left(\frac{1}{2}\right) = \frac{\alpha^2}{2}\,.$$

Consequently, the iteration converges linearly to the solution $r = \frac{1}{2}$ for $\alpha^2 < 2$, and diverges linearly for $\alpha^2 > 2$. Also, (5.58) gives

$$(5.66) \qquad g'(r_\pm) = \frac{4}{\alpha^2} - 1,$$

and therefore, if $\alpha^2 > 2$ then $|g'(r_\pm)| < 1$. Thus, when $\alpha^2 > 2$, the root $r = \frac{1}{2}$ is unstable, while the roots $r_\pm$ are stable for the iteration. Note that convergence is quadratic when $\alpha = 2$, and convergence is slow when α is large.

This example shows that the grid-generation equations can have multiple solutions, and the desired solution can be unstable for a reasonable solution method. These results are verified numerically in §5.4.

5.4. Numerical Experiments

In this section, some results from numerical experiments that were done with the nominal iteration are presented. The numerical code implements a Picard iteration scheme for solving the nonlinear equations; the linear equations are solved using a standard tridiagonal solver. The Picard iterations are run without any relaxation; the iteration is stopped when the maximum of the absolute value of the differences of two successive iterates is less than 10^{-5}. This tolerance is a bit difficult to satisfy, i.e., a fairly large number of iterations are required. On the other hand, a fairly tight tolerance is needed to distinguish multiple solutions near the bifurcation point. Other algorithms were tried (see Steinberg and Roache [65], [66]); none performed as well as the nominal.

First, the results on the problem with one free point are confirmed. Then, larger grids are tested.

5.4.1. Grids With One Free Point.
Table 1 contains the results of some numerical experiments for the parabolas given in (5.1) for various values of α.

TABLE 1

One-point grids.

α	nliter	r	$\tilde{r}$
1.3	46	.49995	.5
1.4	200	.49914	.5
$\sqrt{2}$	—	—	.5
1.5	28	.38221	.38215
2.0	5	.25000	.25000
2.5	11	.20845	.20845
3.0	19	.18820	.18820
5.0	59	.16089	.16088

These results confirm the results in the section on one-point grids, including the bifurcation of the root at $\alpha = \sqrt{2}$. Recall that the grid has two boundary points and one free point. The initial grid contains the points $r = 0.0, 0.01, 1.0$. The initial grid is skewed, so that nonsymmetric solutions will be found. In Table 1, *nliter* is the number of nonlinear iterations, r is the root computed by the numerical code, and $\tilde{r}$ is the true root. Note the increase in the number of iterations as α approaches $\sqrt{2}$ either from above or below. Also, as α increases, the numerical solution is $\frac{1}{2}$ until α passes $\sqrt{2}$, where this root becomes unstable for the iteration and one of the *spurious* roots is computed. Also, note that the iteration count increases as α becomes large, as predicted in §5.3.

5.4.2. Larger Grids. The bifurcation points for the nominal iteration are given in Table 2. The values of α were computed by noting that the number of iterations increases and then decreases as α passes the bifurcation point. Because the grids contain an odd number of points, symmetry implies that the center point for the desired grid should be at the top of the parabola. As α passed through the bifurcation point, this point falls off the top of the parabola. This is illustrated for a 21-point grid in Table 3.

TABLE 2
Bifurcation points.

points	
21	$4.1 < \alpha < 4.2$
41	$5.7 < \alpha < 5.8$
81	$7.6 < \alpha < 7.7$

TABLE 3
Bifurcation point.

α	nlitr	center
4.1	97	.50021
4.15	216	.50094
4.2	71	.51507
4.3	27	.52881
4.5	14	.54408
5.3	18	.57491
5.5	58	.57999

5.5. Comments and Conclusions

The data in Table 2 indicate that the bifurcation point satisfies

(5.67) $$\alpha \approx .8\sqrt{n}.$$

The fact that the bifurcation point grows with the grid resolution is a good feature of the nominal iteration; the nominal iteration's limiting behavior, for high resolution, slowly approaches that of the continuum model.

When numerical experiments are run on the nominal iteration for parameter values above the bifurcation point, a large number of solutions are found, depending on the initial conditions. No pattern of interest is found in the solutions; therefore, these results are not presented.

The fact that the discrete grid-generation equations have multiple solutions is the most important conclusion. Once this is established, changing the method of solving the discrete equations does not help. If the method converges, then the solution found depends on the initial data. What is needed is a new formulation of the grid-generation problem that eliminates the multiple solutions.

The analysis of the continuum grid-generation problem shows that the Euler–Lagrange equation has a unique solution, and this solution is a critical point of the length functional. Moreover, all second-directional derivatives are positive at the critical point, so it is a minimum. In sharp contrast to this, all discrete algorithms studied have a bifurcation after which the solution of the variational problem ceases to be unique.

The one-point grid undergoes a pitchfork bifurcation when the parameter in the example curve is increased. The explicit results given for this problem also provide a check for the numerical codes. The numerical experiments show the true difficulty; the discrete equations have multiple solutions for curves of modest shape and grids that well-resolve the curve.

The analysis done in this paper provides substantial insight into the difficulties (and possible remedies) inherent in the curve and surface grid-generation problem. There is good reason to anticipate analogous problems for solution-adaptive algorithms. Work is now proceeding on developing better algorithms [43].

5.6. Acknowledgments

This work was partially supported by the Office of Naval Research and the Air Force Weapons Laboratory.

Chapter 6

Intrinsic Algebraic Grid Generation

P. M. Knupp

6.1. Introduction

The standard method of algebraic grid generation on planar regions, known as transfinite interpolation, is compared to three new algebraic formulas, termed Alternatives I, II, and III, which are discussed here for the first time. These latter fall into a newly identified class termed *intrinsic* algebraic grid-generation methods. The method of Gilding is shown to be a member of this class. Grids produced with the alternatives are comparable in quality to those obtained by transfinite interpolation. The three alternatives are shown to be tensor products of projectors, rather than Boolean sums, as is the case for transfinite interpolation. In contrast to transfinite interpolation, the grids implied by the alternative methods do not exist for arbitrary regions, but are sensitive to the locations of the four corners of the physical region. The new intrinsic formulas are shown to lack the property of coordinate invariance under affine transformations (translation, rotation, inversion, and stretch). The behavior of Alternative II under translation is examined in detail and shown to be related to the idea of Lagrange interpolation of grids. The existence of a limiting grid (termed the "grid at infinity") is demonstrated for Alternative II; it is shift invariant, and its form is not a tensor product. Finally, a way to exploit the translation property of such algebraic methods using the direct variational method is given.

6.2. Transfinite Interpolation

In the present notation, the well-known transfinite interpolation formula (see [75]) is:

$$x(\xi,\eta) = (1-\eta)x_1(\xi) + \eta x_3(\xi) + (1-\xi)x_2(\eta) + \xi x_4(\eta)$$
$$(6.1) \qquad - \{\xi\eta x_3(1) + \xi(1-\eta)x_1(1) + \eta(1-\xi)x_3(0)$$
$$+ (1-\xi)(1-\eta)x_1(0)\},$$
$$y(\xi,\eta) = (1-\eta)y_1(\xi) + \eta y_3(\xi) + (1-\xi)y_2(\eta) + \xi y_4(\eta)$$

$$(6.2) \qquad - \{\xi\eta y_3(1) + \xi(1-\eta)y_1(1) + \eta(1-\xi)y_3(0)$$
$$+ (1-\xi)(1-\eta)y_1(0)\}.$$

The first-degree Lagrange polynomials $1 - \xi$, ξ, $1 - \eta$, and η are used in this interpolation formula. Using the "corner" identities,

$$(6.3) \qquad (x_1(0), y_1(0)) = (x_2(0), y_2(0)),$$
$$(6.4) \qquad (x_2(1), y_2(1)) = (x_3(0), y_3(0)),$$
$$(6.5) \qquad (x_3(1), y_3(1)) = (x_4(1), y_4(1)),$$
$$(6.6) \qquad (x_4(0), y_4(0)) = (x_1(1), y_1(1)),$$

it is easy to verify that the pair $(x(\xi, \eta), y(\xi, \eta))$ matches the given boundary functions and is continuous on $\overline{U}$, i.e., (x, y) forms a (possibly folded) grid on Ω. Figures 6.1(a), 6.2(a), 6.3(a), and 6.4(a) show grids on four regions generated by this method. The transfinite interpolation grids shown in Figs. 6.2(a) and 6.4(a) are folded. The latter is an example of a grid with a boundary-slope discontinuity; the discontinuity has "propagated" into the interior of the region, as is characteristic of most algebraic systems.

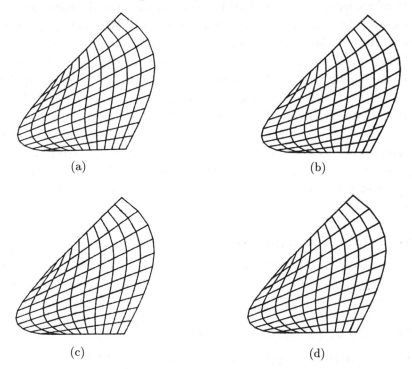

(a)   (b)

(c)   (d)

FIG. 6.1. *Four algebraic grids on a "jar-shaped" region: (a) transfinite interpolation, (b) Gilding's method, (c) Alternative II, and (d) Alternative III.*

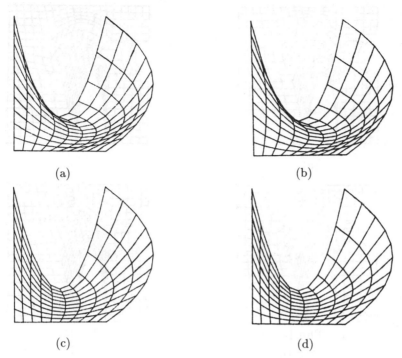

Fig. 6.2. *Four algebraic grids on a "swan-shaped" region: (a) transfinite interpolation, (b) Gilding's method, (c) Alternative II, and (d) Alternative III.*

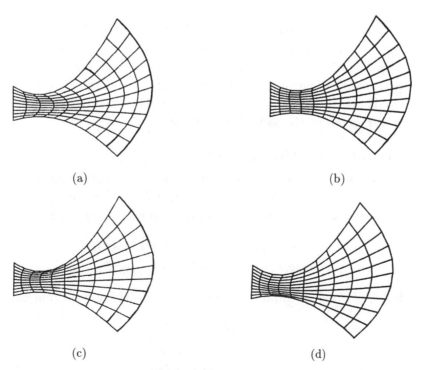

Fig. 6.3. *Four algebraic grids on a "horn-shaped" region: (a) transfinite interpolation, (b) Gilding's method, (c) Alternative II, and (d) Alternative III.*

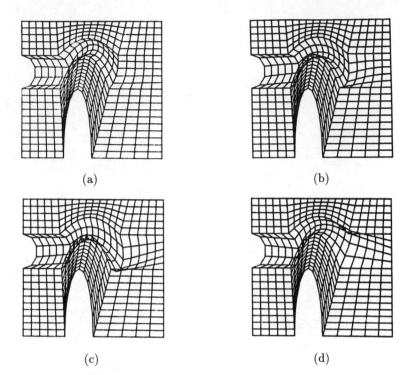

FIG. 6.4. *Four algebraic grids on a "bridgelike" region:* (a) *transfinite interpolation,* (b) *Gilding's method,* (c) *Alternative* II, *and* (d) *Alternative* III.

DEFINITION. An *intrinsic* algebraic grid-generation formula is an algebraic grid formula involving only the boundary functions (including the corners), making no use of "blending" functions. Examples of the "extrinsic" method are the transfinite formulas (6.1) and (6.2), which make use of Lagrange polynomials as blending functions. Examples of intrinsic grid-generation methods are given in the following sections.

6.3. Derivation of Alternative I

The first of the three alternative algebraic grid-generation formulas is derived in this section. Assume the existence of functions $f(\eta)$, $g(\eta)$, $h(\eta)$, and $k(\eta)$ from $0 \leq \eta \leq 1$ to $\mathbf{R}$ such that the continuum grid (x, y) on Ω is given by

$$(6.7) \qquad x(\xi, \eta) = f(\eta)\dot{x}_1(\xi) + g(\eta)x_3(\xi),$$
$$(6.8) \qquad y(\xi, \eta) = h(\eta)y_1(\xi) + k(\eta)y_3(\xi).$$

To find f, g, h, and k, impose the boundary-matching requirements

$$(6.9) \qquad x(0, \eta) = x_2(\eta),$$
$$(6.10) \qquad y(0, \eta) = y_2(\eta),$$
$$(6.11) \qquad x(1, \eta) = x_4(\eta),$$
$$(6.12) \qquad y(1, \eta) = y_4(\eta).$$

This leads to a pair of linear equations for $f(\eta)$ and $g(\eta)$ and another pair for $h(\eta)$ and $k(\eta)$. The solutions to these equations read as follows:

$$(6.13) \qquad f(\eta) = \hat{f}(\eta)/D_1,$$

$$(6.14) \qquad g(\eta) = \hat{g}(\eta)/D_1,$$

$$(6.15) \qquad h(\eta) = \hat{h}(\eta)/D_2,$$

$$(6.16) \qquad k(\eta) = \hat{k}(\eta)/D_2,$$

where

$$(6.17) \qquad \hat{f}(\eta) = \begin{vmatrix} x_2(\eta) & x_3(0) \\ x_4(\eta) & x_3(1) \end{vmatrix},$$

$$(6.18) \qquad \hat{g}(\eta) = \begin{vmatrix} x_1(0) & x_2(\eta) \\ x_1(1) & x_4(\eta) \end{vmatrix},$$

$$(6.19) \qquad D_1 = \begin{vmatrix} x_1(0) & x_3(0) \\ x_1(1) & x_3(1) \end{vmatrix},$$

and similar relations hold for $\hat{h}(\eta)$ and $\hat{k}(\eta)$. Using the "corner identities" (6.4)–(6.6), the pair $(x(\xi, \eta), y(\xi, \eta))$ forms a grid on Ω, since (fortuitously) the full set of boundary-matching conditions are met.

6.4. Derivation of Alternative II

The second alternative algebraic grid-generation formula is derived, being formulated in terms of complex variables. The alternative is shown to be a bilinear form. The real and imaginary parts of the second alternative are also derived. Let $z(\xi, \eta) = x(\xi, \eta) + \imath y(\xi, \eta)$ and $z_1(\xi) = x_1(\xi) + \imath y_1(\xi)$, etc. Assume $z(\xi, \eta)$ to have the form

$$(6.20) \qquad z(\xi, \eta) = f(\eta)z_1(\xi) + g(\eta)z_3(\xi),$$

where $f(\eta)$ and $g(\eta)$ map U_1 (the unit interval $0 \leq \eta \leq 1$) to $\mathbf{C}$. Imposing boundary-matching conditions gives $f(\eta) = \hat{f}(\eta)/D_{\mathrm{II}}$ and $g(\eta) = \hat{g}(\eta)/D_{\mathrm{II}}$, where

$$(6.21) \qquad D_{II} = \begin{vmatrix} z_1(0) & z_3(0) \\ z_1(1) & z_3(1) \end{vmatrix}$$

and

$$(6.22) \qquad \hat{f}(\eta) = \begin{vmatrix} z_2(\eta) & z_3(0) \\ z_4(\eta) & z_3(1) \end{vmatrix},$$

$$(6.23) \qquad \hat{g}(\eta) = \begin{vmatrix} z_1(0) & z_2(\eta) \\ z_1(1) & z_4(\eta) \end{vmatrix}.$$

Then $z(\xi, \eta)$ forms a grid, since (again fortuitously) the boundary-matching conditions hold. Figures 6.1(c), 6.2(c), 6.3(c), and 6.4(c) show grids generated with this method. The grid in 6.2(c) is nonfolded, but 6.4(c) remains folded. The form for this grid is symmetric in that if the form

$$(6.24) \qquad z(\xi, \eta) = \phi(\xi)z_2(\eta) + \psi(\xi)z_4(\eta)$$

is assumed instead of (6.20), the same grid results.

The expressions for Alternative II are simplified if the determinants for $\hat{f}(\eta)$ and $\hat{g}(\eta)$ are expanded and substituted into the formula (6.20) to get

$$z(\xi, \eta) = \frac{1}{D_{\mathrm{II}}}\{z_3(1)z_2(\eta)z_1(\xi) - z_3(0)z_4(\eta)z_1(\xi)$$

$$(6.25) \qquad\qquad + z_1(0)z_4(\eta)z_3(\xi) - z_1(1)z_2(\eta)z_3(\xi)\}.$$

If we let $\tilde{M}$ be the matrix with the following elements in $\mathbf{C}$:

$$(6.26) \qquad \tilde{M} = \begin{pmatrix} z_3(1) & -z_3(0) \\ -z_1(1) & z_1(0) \end{pmatrix},$$

and $u(\xi) = (z_1(\xi), z_3(\xi))$, $v(\eta) = (z_2(\eta), z_4(\eta)) \in \mathbf{C} \times \mathbf{C}$, then (6.25) may be written as

$$(6.27) \qquad D_{\mathrm{II}}z(\xi, \eta) = u(\xi)\tilde{M}v^T(\eta),$$

where $D_{\mathrm{II}} = \det \tilde{M}$. The grid z is then seen to be a bilinear form in u and v. Alternatives I and III (see §6.5) may also be expressed as bilinear forms similar to (6.27).

Alternative II may be separated into real and imaginary parts using the following lemma.

LEMMA 6.4.1. *Let $\tilde{Z}$ and $\tilde{W}$ be two 2×2 matrices with elements in $\mathbf{C}$:*

$$(6.28) \qquad \tilde{Z} = \begin{pmatrix} x_1 + \imath y_1 & x_2 + \imath y_2 \\ x_3 + \imath y_3 & x_4 + \imath y_4 \end{pmatrix},$$

$$(6.29) \qquad \tilde{W} = \begin{pmatrix} u_1 + \imath v_1 & u_2 + \imath v_2 \\ u_3 + \imath v_3 & u_4 + \imath v_4 \end{pmatrix}.$$

If $u_2 = x_2$, $v_2 = y_2$, $u_4 = x_4$, and $v_4 = y_4$, then

$$(6.30) \qquad \Re\{\det(Z\overline{W})\} = \begin{vmatrix} u_1 & -y_1 & x_2 & -y_2 \\ v_1 & x_1 & y_2 & x_2 \\ u_3 & -y_3 & x_4 & -y_4 \\ v_3 & x_3 & y_4 & x_4 \end{vmatrix},$$

$$(6.31) \qquad \Im\{\det(Z\overline{W})\} = \begin{vmatrix} x_1 & u_1 & x_2 & -y_2 \\ y_1 & v_1 & y_2 & x_2 \\ x_3 & u_3 & x_4 & -y_4 \\ y_3 & v_3 & y_4 & x_4 \end{vmatrix}.$$

Proof. The proof of this lemma is a direct computation. $\qquad\square$

COROLLARY 6.4.1.

$$(6.32) \qquad \det(Z\overline{Z}) = \begin{vmatrix} x_1 & -y_1 & x_2 & -y_2 \\ y_1 & x_1 & y_2 & x_2 \\ x_3 & -y_3 & x_4 & -y_4 \\ y_3 & x_3 & y_4 & x_4 \end{vmatrix}.$$

THEOREM 6.4.1. *Alternative* II *may also be expressed as*

$$(6.33) \qquad x(\xi,\eta) = a_1(\eta)x_1(\xi) - b_1(\eta)y_1(\xi) + a_2(\eta)x_3(\xi) - b_2(\eta)y_3(\xi),$$
$$(6.34) \qquad y(\xi,\eta) = b_1(\eta)x_1(\xi) + a_1(\eta)y_1(\xi) + b_2(\eta)x_3(\xi) + a_2(\eta)y_3(\xi),$$

where $a_1(\eta) = \hat{a}_1(\eta)/D$, $a_2(\eta) = \hat{a}_2(\eta)/D$, $b_1(\eta) = \hat{b}_1(\eta)/D$, *and* $b_2(\eta) = \hat{b}_2(\eta)/D$, *and*

$$(6.35) \qquad D = \begin{vmatrix} x_1(0) & -y_1(0) & x_3(0) & -y_3(0) \\ y_1(0) & x_1(0) & y_3(0) & x_3(0) \\ x_1(1) & -y_1(1) & x_3(1) & -y_3(1) \\ y_1(1) & x_1(1) & y_3(1) & x_3(1) \end{vmatrix},$$

$$(6.36) \qquad \hat{a}_1(\eta) = \begin{vmatrix} x_2(\eta) & -y_1(0) & x_3(0) & -y_3(0) \\ y_2(\eta) & x_1(0) & y_3(0) & x_3(0) \\ x_4(\eta) & -y_1(1) & x_3(1) & -y_3(1) \\ y_4(\eta) & x_1(1) & y_3(1) & x_3(1) \end{vmatrix},$$

$$(6.37) \qquad \hat{b}_1(\eta) = \begin{vmatrix} x_1(0) & x_2(\eta) & x_3(0) & -y_3(0) \\ y_1(0) & y_2(\eta) & y_3(0) & x_3(0) \\ x_1(1) & x_4(\eta) & x_3(1) & -y_3(1) \\ y_1(1) & y_4(\eta) & y_3(1) & x_3(1) \end{vmatrix},$$

$$(6.38) \qquad \hat{a}_2(\eta) = \begin{vmatrix} x_1(0) & -y_1(0) & x_2(\eta) & -y_3(0) \\ y_1(0) & x_1(0) & y_2(\eta) & x_3(0) \\ x_1(1) & -y_1(1) & x_4(\eta) & -y_3(1) \\ y_1(1) & x_1(1) & y_4(\eta) & x_3(1) \end{vmatrix},$$

$$(6.39) \qquad \hat{b}_2(\eta) = \begin{vmatrix} x_1(0) & -y_1(0) & x_3(0) & x_2(\eta) \\ y_1(0) & x_1(0) & y_3(0) & y_2(\eta) \\ x_1(1) & -y_1(1) & x_3(1) & x_4(\eta) \\ y_1(1) & x_1(1) & y_3(1) & y_4(\eta) \end{vmatrix}.$$

Proof. Equation (6.20) may be written as

$$(6.40) \qquad z(\xi,\eta) = \frac{\overline{D}_{\text{II}}\hat{f}z_1 + \overline{D}_{\text{II}}\hat{g}z_3}{D_{\text{II}}\overline{D}_{\text{II}}}.$$

Applying (6.32) to the denominator results in $D_{\text{II}}\overline{D}_{\text{II}} = D$, where D is defined in (6.35). Also,

(6.41)
$$\Re(\overline{D}_{\mathrm{II}}\hat{f}z_1) = \Re(\det(Z\overline{W})),$$

where

(6.42)
$$Z = \begin{pmatrix} z_1(0)z_1(\xi) & z_3(0) \\ z_1(1)z_1(\xi) & z_3(1) \end{pmatrix},$$

(6.43)
$$\overline{W} = \begin{pmatrix} z_2(\eta) & z_3(0) \\ z_4(\eta) & a_3(1) \end{pmatrix}.$$

Applying (6.30) gives

(6.44)
$$\mathrm{Re}(\overline{D}_{\mathrm{II}}\hat{f}z_1) = x_1(\xi)\hat{a}_1(\eta) - y_1(\xi)\hat{b}_1(\eta).$$

The other two terms in (6.34) are derived from $\Re(\overline{D}_{\mathrm{II}}\hat{g}z_3)$, and (6.34) is derived from the imaginary parts in a similar manner.   □
     The relations (6.35)–(6.39) could also be derived by assuming the forms (6.33) and (6.34) at the beginning and applying the boundary-matching conditions.

6.5. Derivation of Alternative III

The third alternative formula is derived and an extension to curves in R^3 is given. Assume the existence of functions $a_1(\eta)$, $b_1(\eta)$, $a_3(\eta)$, and $b_3(\eta)$ from U_1 to $\mathbf{R}$ such that the grid $x(\xi,\eta)$, $y(\xi,\eta)$ has the form

(6.45) $x(\xi,\eta) = a_1(\eta)x_1(\xi) + b_1(\eta)y_1(\xi) + a_3(\eta)x_3(\xi) + b_3(\eta)y_3(\xi),$

(6.46) $y(\xi,\eta) = a_1(\eta)y_1(\xi) + b_1(\eta)x_1(\xi) + a_3(\eta)y_3(\xi) + b_3(\eta)x_3(\xi).$

Applying the usual boundary-matching conditions, one finds

(6.47)
$$a_1(\eta) = \frac{\hat{a}_1(\eta)}{D},$$

(6.48)
$$b_1(\eta) = \frac{\hat{b}_1(\eta)}{D},$$

(6.49)
$$a_3(\eta) = \frac{\hat{a}_3(\eta)}{D},$$

(6.50)
$$b_3(\eta) = \frac{\hat{b}_3(\eta)}{D},$$

where

(6.51)
$$D = \begin{vmatrix} x_1(0) & y_1(0) & x_3(0) & y_3(0) \\ y_1(0) & x_1(0) & y_3(0) & x_3(0) \\ x_1(1) & y_1(1) & x_3(1) & y_3(1) \\ y_1(1) & x_1(1) & y_3(1) & x_3(1) \end{vmatrix}$$

and

$$(6.52) \quad \hat{a}_1(\eta) = \begin{vmatrix} x_2(\eta) & y_1(0) & x_3(0) & y_3(0) \\ y_2(\eta) & x_1(0) & y_3(0) & x_3(0) \\ x_4(\eta) & y_1(1) & x_3(1) & y_3(1) \\ y_4(\eta) & x_1(1) & y_3(1) & x_3(1) \end{vmatrix},$$

$$(6.53) \quad \hat{b}_1(\eta) = \begin{vmatrix} x_1(0) & x_2(\eta) & x_3(0) & y_3(0) \\ y_1(0) & y_2(\eta) & y_3(0) & x_3(0) \\ x_1(1) & x_4(\eta) & x_3(1) & y_3(1) \\ y_1(1) & y_4(\eta) & y_3(1) & x_3(1) \end{vmatrix},$$

$$(6.54) \quad \hat{a}_3(\eta) = \begin{vmatrix} x_1(0) & y_1(0) & x_2(\eta) & y_3(0) \\ y_1(0) & x_1(0) & y_2(\eta) & x_3(0) \\ x_1(1) & y_1(1) & x_4(\eta) & y_3(1) \\ y_1(1) & x_1(1) & y_4(\eta) & x_3(1) \end{vmatrix},$$

$$(6.55) \quad \hat{b}_3(\eta) = \begin{vmatrix} x_1(0) & y_1(0) & x_3(0) & x_2(\eta) \\ y_1(0) & x_1(0) & y_3(0) & y_2(\eta) \\ x_1(1) & y_1(1) & x_3(1) & x_4(\eta) \\ y_1(1) & x_1(1) & y_3(1) & y_4(\eta) \end{vmatrix}.$$

Figures 6.1(d), 6.2(d), 6.3(d), and 6.4(d) show grids generated by Alternative III. They are similar to those generated by Alternative II.

This alternative can be extended to fit four curved boundaries in R^3 by generalizing to the form

$$(6.56) \quad \begin{aligned} x(\xi, \eta) &= a_1(\eta)x_1(\xi) + b_1(\eta)z_1(\xi) + c_1(\eta)y_1(\xi) \\ &\quad + a_3(\eta)x_3(\xi) + b_3(\eta)z_3(\xi) + c_3(\eta)y_3(\xi), \end{aligned}$$

$$(6.57) \quad \begin{aligned} y(\xi, \eta) &= a_1(\eta)y_1(\xi) + b_1(\eta)x_1(\xi) + c_1(\eta)z_1(\xi) \\ &\quad + a_3(\eta)y_3(\xi) + b_3(\eta)x_3(\xi) + c_3(\eta)z_3(\xi), \end{aligned}$$

$$(6.58) \quad \begin{aligned} z(\xi, \eta) &= a_1(\eta)z_1(\xi) + b_1(\eta)y_1(\xi) + c_1(\eta)x_1(\xi) \\ &\quad + a_3(\eta)z_3(\xi) + b_3(\eta)y_3(\xi) + c_3(\eta)x_3(\xi) \end{aligned}$$

and applying boundary-matching conditions. This procedure results in 6×6 determinants for the unknown functions. Note that the interior is determined by the boundary functions and so cannot be used to grid an arbitrary surface. However, this limitation is true of the analogous transfinite interpolation formula as well. In general, there appear to be no intrinsic algebraic formulas for hexahedral volumes in R^3.

6.6. Gilding's Method

For comparison with the alternatives presented so far, Gilding's method [34] of intrinsic algebraic grid generation is introduced. Translated into the present notation, Gilding's formula reads:

$$x(\xi,\eta) = [\{x_\alpha(\xi,\eta)\delta_x(\eta) + y_\alpha(\xi,\eta)\delta_y(\eta)\}\epsilon_y(\xi)$$
(6.59)
$$- \{x_\beta(\xi,\eta)\epsilon_x(\xi) + y_\beta(\xi,\eta)\epsilon_y(\xi)\}\delta_y(\eta)]/\Delta(\xi,\eta),$$
$$y(\xi,\eta) = [\{x_\beta(\xi,\eta)\epsilon_x(\xi) + y_\beta(\xi,\eta)\epsilon_y(\xi)\}\delta_x(\eta)$$
(6.60)
$$- \{x_\alpha(\xi,\eta)\delta_x(\eta) + y_\alpha(\xi,\eta)\delta_y(\eta)\}\epsilon_x(\xi)]/\Delta(\xi,\eta),$$

where

(6.61)
$$\Delta(\xi,\eta) = \delta_x(\eta)\epsilon_y(\xi) - \epsilon_x(\xi)\delta_y(\eta),$$

(6.62)
$$x_\alpha(\xi,\eta) = x_2(\eta) + \alpha(\xi,\eta)\delta_x(\eta),$$

(6.63)
$$y_\alpha(\xi,\eta) = y_2(\eta) + \alpha(\xi,\eta)\delta_y(\eta),$$

(6.64)
$$x_\beta(\xi,\eta) = x_1(\xi) + \beta(\xi,\eta)\epsilon_x(\xi),$$

(6.65)
$$y_\beta(\xi,\eta) = y_1(\xi) + \beta(\xi,\eta)\epsilon_y(\xi)$$

and

(6.66)
$$\alpha(\xi,\eta) = [\{1 - \beta_1(\eta)\}\alpha_1(\xi) + \beta_1(\eta)\alpha_2(\xi)]/d(\xi,\eta),$$

(6.67)
$$\beta(\xi,\eta) = [\{1 - \alpha_1(\xi)\}\beta_1(\eta) + \alpha_1(\xi)\beta_2(\eta)]/d(\xi,\eta),$$

(6.68)
$$d(\xi,\eta) = 1 - [\alpha_2(\xi) - \alpha_1(\xi)][\beta_2(\eta) - \beta_1(\eta)],$$

(6.69)
$$\alpha_1(\xi) = \frac{[x_1(\xi) - x_1(0)][x_4(0) - x_2(0)] + [y_1(\xi) - y_1(0)][y_4(0) - y_2(0)]}{\delta_x^2(0) + \delta_y^2(0)},$$

(6.70)
$$\alpha_2(\xi) = \frac{[x_3(\xi) - x_3(0)][x_4(1) - x_2(1)] + [y_3(\xi) - y_3(0)][y_4(1) - y_2(1)]}{\delta_x^2(1) + \delta_y^2(1)},$$

(6.71)
$$\beta_1(\eta) = \frac{[x_2(\eta) - x_2(0)][x_3(0) - x_1(0)] + [y_2(\eta) - y_2(0)][y_3(0) - y_1(0)]}{\epsilon_x^2(0) + \epsilon_y^2(0)},$$

(6.72)
$$\beta_2(\eta) = \frac{[x_4(\eta) - x_4(0)][x_3(1) - x_1(1)] + [y_4(\eta) - y_4(0)][y_3(1) - y_1(1)]}{\epsilon_x^2(1) + \epsilon_y^2(1)},$$

with

(6.73) $\delta_x(\eta) = x_4(\eta) - x_2(\eta),$

(6.74) $\delta_y(\eta) = y_4(\eta) - y_2(\eta),$

(6.75) $\epsilon_x(\xi) = x_3(\xi) - x_1(\xi),$

(6.76) $\epsilon_y(\xi) = y_3(\xi) - y_1(\xi).$

Since the divisors $\Delta(\xi, \eta)$ and $d(\xi, \eta)$ are functions of ξ and η, it is evident that Gilding's method is distinct from the three previous alternative algebraic grid-generation methods; however, it is yet another example of an intrinsic method, since it makes no use of blending functions. The complexity of the formulas (6.59) and (6.60) makes it doubtful that Gilding's method could be derived by assuming a simple form, as was done in obtaining Alternative I–III. Figures 6.1(b), 6.2(b), 6.3(b), and 6.4(b) show grids generated by Gilding's method. The grids are similar to those generated by transfinite interpolation.

6.7. Existence of the Grids

In this section, it is shown that the intrinsic methods do not always exist on arbitrary regions. The transfinite grid-generation formula puts no restrictions on the boundary functions comprising $\partial\Omega$, thus the grid exists for any region. This is not the case for the intrinsic methods. Grids produced by Alternative I exist only if D_1 (6.19) and D_2 are both not zero. The method will succeed or fail to produce a grid, depending on the location of the four corner points of the region Ω, rather than on the four boundary curves. If $D_1 = 0$, then either there exist multiple solutions for $f(\eta)$ and $g(\eta)$ (as in the case of the unit square) or there exist no solutions, in which case no grid may be constructed by this method. Because Alternative I fails to exist for the unit square, as well as many other regions of interest, it is not studied further.

A similar, but somewhat better, situation holds for Alternative II; grids may be generated by this method provided $D_{II} \neq 0$. Alternative II produces the standard grid $x(\xi, \eta) = \xi$, $y(\xi, \eta) = \eta$ on the unit square.

THEOREM 6.7.1. *Let $z_1(0) \neq 0$. Then $D_{II} = 0$ if and only if*

(6.77) $$w_3 = \frac{w_1 w_2}{z_1(0)} + w_1 + w_2,$$

where $w_3 = z_3(1) - z_1(0)$, $w_1 = z_3(0) - z_1(0)$, and $w_2 = z_1(1) - z_1(0)$. If $z_1(0) = 0$, then $D_{II} = 0$ if and only if $w_1 = 0$ or $w_2 = 0$.

The proof involves nothing more than straightforward algebra. Since D_{II} depends on the corner point $z_1(0)$, as well as on the difference of corner points, it is seen that the value of D_{II} is dependent not only on the geometric shape of the quadrilateral formed by the corner points, but also upon the location of Ω in the plane. Therefore, D_{II} in Alternative II can be zero for many regions Ω. Fortunately, $D_{II} \neq 0$ for many regions of interest as well. From (6.51), it is seen that a similar situation must hold for Alternative III. Gilding's method may also fail to create a grid on certain regions [34].

6.8. Comparison of the Methods

So far, five methods of algebraic grid generation have been presented, three original ones, and two previously known. It is desirable to compare the various methods to determine their strengths and weaknesses. For highly symmetric regions Ω all of the methods may produce the same or a similar grid. For example, if Ω is the unit square, the standard grid $x(\xi,\eta) = \xi$, $y(\xi,\eta) = \eta$ is produced by transfinite interpolation, Alternative II, Alternative III, and Gilding's method. Alternative I also produces this grid, but with multiple solutions for the $f(\eta)$ and $g(\eta)$.

A sufficient condition on Ω that ensures identical grids for transfinite interpolation and the three Alternatives is that two opposite sides of Ω are straight lines. Then, all four methods reduce to the " shearing transformation":

$$(6.78) \qquad x(\xi,\eta) = (1 - \xi)x_2(\eta) + \xi x_4(\eta),$$

$$(6.79) \qquad y(\xi,\eta) = (1 - \xi)y_2(\eta) + \xi y_4(\eta).$$

However, Gilding's method does not reduce to the shearing transformation under this assumption. Necessary conditions for the equivalence of these methods are not geometrically illuminating.

On the other hand, the various methods can produce different grids for a given region Ω. For example, let Ω be the region in Fig. 6.5 given by

$$(6.80) \qquad x_1(\xi) = \xi + \rho(\xi),$$

$$(6.81) \qquad y_1(\xi) = \tau(\xi),$$

$$(6.82) \qquad x_3(\xi) = \xi,$$

$$(6.83) \qquad y_3(\xi) = 1,$$

$$(6.84) \qquad x_2(\eta) = \tilde{\rho}(\eta),$$

$$(6.85) \qquad y_2(\eta) = \eta + \tilde{\tau}(\eta),$$

$$(6.86) \qquad x_4(\eta) = 1,$$

$$(6.87) \qquad y_4(\eta) = \eta$$

where ρ, τ, $\tilde{\rho}$, and $\tilde{\tau}$ are arbitrary except for the end conditions $\rho(0) = 0$, $\tau(0) = 0$, $\rho(1) = 0$, $\tau(1) = 0$, $\tilde{\rho}(0) = 0$, $\tilde{\tau}(0) = 0$, $\tilde{\rho}(1) = 0$, and $\tilde{\tau}(1) = 0$. On this region, transfinite interpolation produces the grid

$$(6.88) \qquad x(\xi,\eta) = \xi + (1 - \eta)\rho(\xi) + (1 - \xi)\tilde{\rho}(\eta),$$

$$(6.89) \qquad y(\xi,\eta) = \eta + (1 - \eta)\tau(\xi) + (1 - \xi)\tilde{\tau}(\eta).$$

Alternative I fails since $D_1 = 0$. Alternative II gives

$$(6.90) \qquad \begin{aligned} x(\xi,\eta) = {} & \xi + (1 - \eta)\rho(\xi) + (1 - \xi)\tilde{\rho}(\eta) \\ & - \tau(\xi)\tilde{\rho}(\eta) + \tau(\xi)\tilde{\tau}(\eta) - \rho(\xi)\tilde{\rho}(\eta) - \rho(\xi)\tilde{\tau}(\eta), \end{aligned}$$

$$(6.91) \qquad \begin{aligned} y(\xi,\eta) = {} & \eta + (1 - \eta)\tau(\xi) + (1 - \xi)\tilde{\tau}(\eta) \\ & - \tau(\xi)\tilde{\rho}(\eta) - \tau(\xi)\tilde{\tau}(\eta) + \rho(\xi)\tilde{\rho}(\eta) - \rho(\xi)\tilde{\tau}(\eta) \end{aligned}$$

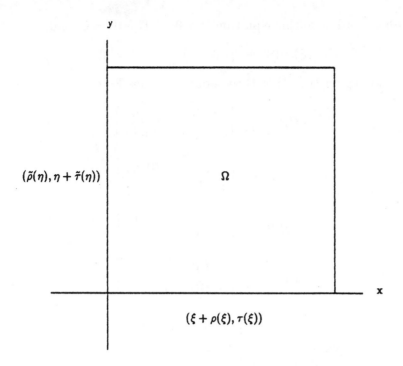

FIG. 6.5. *A small perturbation of the logical square.*

whereas Alternative III gives the following set of equations:

$$x(\xi, \eta) = \xi + (1 - \eta)\rho(\xi) + (1 - \xi)\tilde{\rho}(\eta)$$

(6.92)
$$- \tau(\xi)\tilde{\rho}(\eta) - \tau(\xi)\tilde{\tau}(\eta) - \rho(\xi)\tilde{\rho}(\eta) - \rho(\xi)\tilde{\tau}(\eta),$$

$$y(\xi, \eta) = \eta + (1 - \eta)\tau(\xi) + (1 - \xi)\tilde{\tau}(\eta)$$

(6.93)
$$- \tau(\xi)\tilde{\rho}(\eta) - \tau(\xi)\tilde{\tau}(\eta) - \rho(\xi)\tilde{\rho}(\eta) - \rho(\xi)\tilde{\tau}(\eta).$$

Gilding's formula for this region is very long and complex (and not worth recording); it is clearly different from both the transfinite interpolation and the Alternative formulas I–III. Gilding's method can even produce grids different from the other methods when three of the boundaries of Ω are straight lines (e.g., consider the previous example with $\rho(\xi) = \xi$ and $\tau(\xi) = 0$).

6.9. Periodic "Blending" Functions

The three alternative algebraic methods were derived by assuming a form and matching the boundary functions to the form. If this is attempted for transfinite interpolation, the approach fails. Assume that the mapping function $x(\xi, \eta)$ has the form

(6.94) $\quad x(\xi, \eta) = a(\eta)x_1(\xi) + b(\eta)x_3(\xi) + c(\xi)x_2(\eta) + d(\xi)x_4(\eta) + e(\xi, \eta).$

Application of the boundary-matching condition at $\eta = 0$ results in

(6.95) $\quad x_1(\xi) = a(0)x_1(\xi) + b(0)x_3(\xi) + c(\xi)x_2(0) + d(\xi)x_4(0) + e(\xi, 0).$

The obvious solution to this equation is $a(0) = 1$, $b(0) = 0$, and

$$(6.96) \qquad c(\xi)x_2(0) + d(\xi)x_4(0) + e(\xi, 0) = 0.$$

Similar reasoning on the other three boundaries leads to

$$(6.97) \qquad a(\eta) = \frac{1}{D_3} \begin{vmatrix} -e(0,\eta) & x_3(0) \\ -e(1,\eta) & x_3(1) \end{vmatrix},$$

$$(6.98) \qquad b(\eta) = \frac{1}{D_3} \begin{vmatrix} x_1(0) & -e(0,\eta) \\ x_1(1) & -e(1,\eta) \end{vmatrix},$$

$$(6.99) \qquad c(\eta) = \frac{1}{D_3} \begin{vmatrix} -e(\xi,0) & x_1(1) \\ -e(\xi,1) & x_3(1) \end{vmatrix},$$

$$(6.100) \qquad d(\eta) = \frac{1}{D_3} \begin{vmatrix} x_1(0) & -e(\xi,0) \\ x_3(0) & -e(\xi,1) \end{vmatrix},$$

where

$$(6.101) \qquad D_3 = \begin{vmatrix} x_1(0) & x_3(0) \\ x_1(1) & x_3(1) \end{vmatrix}.$$

The function $e(\xi, \eta)$ is indeterminate, except at the corners, where it is required that the following equations hold true:

$$(6.102) \qquad e(0,0) = -x_1(0),$$
$$(6.103) \qquad e(1,0) = -x_1(1),$$
$$(6.104) \qquad e(0,1) = -x_3(0),$$
$$(6.105) \qquad e(1,1) = -x_3(1).$$

In general, then, the assumed system (6.94) will be satisfied if $e(\xi, \eta)$ has the form

$$(6.106) \qquad \begin{aligned} -e(\xi, \eta) = {} & h(\xi)f(\eta)x_3(1) + h(\xi)g(\eta)x_1(1) \\ & + k(\xi)f(\eta)x_3(0) + k(\xi)g(\eta)x_1(0), \end{aligned}$$

where the "cardinality conditions" $h(0) = 0$, $h(1) = 1$, $f(0) = 0$, $f(1) = 1$, $k(0) = 1$, $k(1) = 0$, $g(0) = 1$, and $g(1) = 0$ are satisfied. The form (6.94) therefore leads to a nonintrinsic method in that $e(\xi, \eta)$ is not completely determined by the boundary functions. The transfinite interpolation formula (6.1) results when $h(\xi) = \xi$, $f(\eta) = \eta$, $k(\xi) = 1 - \xi$, $g(\eta) = 1 - \eta$.

The choice of a periodic set of blending functions satisfying the cardinality conditions leads to the following equation:

$$(6.107) \quad x(\xi, \eta) = \cos\left(\frac{\pi}{2}\eta\right) x_1(\xi) + \sin\left(\frac{\pi}{2}\eta\right) x_3(\xi) + \cos\left(\frac{\pi}{2}\xi\right) x_2(\eta)$$

$$+ \sin\left(\frac{\pi}{2}\xi\right) x_4(\eta) - e(\xi, \eta),$$

where

(6.108)
$$e(\xi, \eta) = \sin\left(\frac{\pi}{2}\xi\right)\sin\left(\frac{\pi}{2}\eta\right)x_3(1) + \sin\left(\frac{\pi}{2}\xi\right)\cos\left(\frac{\pi}{2}\eta\right)x_1(1)$$
$$+ \cos\left(\frac{\pi}{2}\xi\right)\sin\left(\frac{\pi}{2}\eta\right)x_3(0) + \cos\left(\frac{\pi}{2}\xi\right)\cos\left(\frac{\pi}{2}\eta\right)x_1(0).$$

A similar relation for $y(\xi, \eta)$ is obtained by replacing x with y in these equations. The resulting algebraic grid-generation formula possesses several unattractive features: (i) it does not reduce to $x(\xi, \eta) = \xi$, $y(\xi, \eta) = \eta$ on the unit square, (ii) it does not reduce to the "shearing transformation" when opposite sides of Ω are straight-line segments, and (iii) it is not shift invariant. In §6.12, it is shown how some of these features can be turned to advantage.

It is noted in passing that the "periodic" transfinite interpolation formula is the solution to the following partial differential equation:

(6.109)
$$x_{\xi\xi\eta\eta} + \frac{\pi^2}{4}(x_{\xi\xi} + x_{\eta\eta}) + \frac{\pi^4}{16}x = 0.$$

For comparison, the transfinite interpolation formula with first degree Lagrange polynomial blending functions is known [75] to satisfy $x_{\xi\xi\eta\eta} = 0$.

6.10. Algebraic Methods under Coordinate Transformations

The intrinsic methods do not exhibit the properties of translation, rotation, and stretch invariance that are expected in a grid-generation method. To describe this behavior in detail, the invariance properties are defined for algebraic grid-generation methods. The invariance properties of all known algebraic methods are cataloged.

Given the four boundary curves $z_1(\xi), z_2(\eta), z_3(\xi), z_4(\eta)$, let $z(\xi, \eta)$ be a grid on Ω generated by some algebraic method.

(i) Let $z_0 \in \mathbf{C}$ be added to every point of $\partial\Omega$ so that the new boundary is

(6.110) $$z_1'(\xi) = z_1(\xi) + z_0,$$
(6.111) $$z_2'(\eta) = z_2(\eta) + z_0,$$
(6.112) $$z_3'(\xi) = z_3(\xi) + z_0,$$
(6.113) $$z_4'(\eta) = z_4(\eta) + z_0,$$

and let $z'(\xi, \eta)$ be the grid generated from the shifted boundary curves by the same method as was the original grid $z(\xi, \eta)$. Then the grid-generation method is *shift invariant* if

(6.114) $$z'(\xi, \eta) = z(\xi, \eta) + z_0$$

for all $\xi, \eta \in U_2$ and all $z_0 \in \mathbf{C}$ (equivalently, $\partial z'/\partial z_0 = 1$);

(ii) Let every point of $\partial\Omega$ be multiplied by $e^{i\theta}$ with $0 \leq \theta \leq 2\pi$, so that the new boundary functions are $z_1'(\xi) = e^{i\theta}z_1(\xi)$, etc. Then the grid-generation method is *rotationally invariant* if

(6.115) $$z'(\xi, \eta) = e^{i\theta}z(\xi, \eta)$$

for all $\xi, \eta \in U_2$ (equivalently, $\partial^2 z' / \partial \theta^2 = -z'$);

(iii) Let $\partial \Omega$ be "flipped" about the x-axis by the operation

$$(6.116) \qquad z_1'(\xi) = \overline{z}_1(\xi),$$

$$(6.117) \qquad z_2'(\eta) = \overline{z}_2(\eta),$$

$$(6.118) \qquad z_3'(\xi) = \overline{z}_3(\xi),$$

$$(6.119) \qquad z_4'(\eta) = \overline{z}_4(\eta).$$

Then the grid-generation method is *mirror flip invariant* about the x-axis if $z'(\xi, \eta) = \overline{z}(\xi, \eta)$. A flip about the y-axis is defined similarly, e.g., $z_1'(\xi) = -\overline{z}_1(\xi)$, $z_2'(\eta) = -\overline{z}_2(\eta)$, etc., so that $z'(\xi, \eta) = -\overline{z}(\xi, \eta)$ is required for y-mirror flip invariance;

(iv) Let $\partial \Omega$ be uniformly stretched by $r \in R^+$:

$$(6.120) \qquad z_1'(\xi) = r z_1(\xi),$$

$$(6.121) \qquad z_2'(\eta) = r z_2(\eta),$$

$$(6.122) \qquad z_3'(\xi) = r z_3(\xi),$$

$$(6.123) \qquad z_4'(\eta) = r z_4(\eta).$$

Then the grid-generation method is *stretch invariant* if $z'(\xi, \eta) = r z(\xi, \eta)$. Most grid-generation methods proposed to date are, in fact, invariant under all the above transformations. However, the alternatives are not invariant in some cases, as shown in Table 6.1 (a "Yes" entry in the table means that the method is invariant under the given transformation).

TABLE 6.1
Invariance properties of algebraic methods.

Algebraic Method	Shift	Rotation	Flip	Stretch
Shearing (78, 79)	Yes	Yes	Yes	Yes
TFI (1, 2)	Yes	Yes	Yes	Yes
Periodic (107–108)	No	Yes	Yes	Yes
AI (7, 8)	No	No	Yes	Yes
AII (20)	No	Yes	Yes	Yes
AIII (45, 46)	No	No	Yes	Yes
z_∞ (127)	Yes	Yes	Yes	Yes
Gilding (59, 60)	Yes	Yes	Yes	Yes

6.11. Alternative II under a Shift

In this section, the shifted grid for Alternative II is analyzed in detail. It is shown that the shifted grid may be expressed in terms of a linear combination of two algebraic forms $A(\xi, \eta)$ and $B(\xi, \eta)$. A new algebraic formula for grid generation, termed the "grid at infinity," is obtained by letting the shift parameter tend to infinity. Properties of the "grid at infinity" are explored. Finally, it is shown that the shifted grid in Alternative II is related to Lagrange interpolation between the unshifted grid and the "grid at infinity."

Let $\zeta \in \mathbf{C}$. Consider the grid $z(\xi, \eta; \zeta)$ obtained from Alternative II when the boundary values are shifted by adding ζ. Let the "restored grid," obtained by shifting $z(\xi, \eta; \zeta)$ back to the original location, be $z_R(\xi, \eta; \zeta) = z(\xi, \eta; \zeta) - \zeta$.

THEOREM 6.11.1. *The restored grid may be expressed as*

$$(6.124) \qquad z_R(\xi, \eta; \zeta) = \frac{B(\xi, \eta) + \zeta A(\xi, \eta)}{D_{\mathrm{II}} + \zeta E_{\mathrm{II}}}$$

where $E_{\mathrm{II}} = z_3(1) + z_1(0) - z_3(0) - z_1(1)$,

$$(6.125) \qquad \begin{aligned} B(\xi, \eta) &= z_3(1)z_2(\eta)z_1(\xi) - z_3(0)z_4(\eta)z_1(\xi) \\ &\quad + z_1(0)z_4(\eta)z_3(\xi) - z_1(1)z_2(\eta)z_3(\xi), \end{aligned}$$

and

$$(6.126) \qquad \begin{aligned} A(\xi, \eta) &= [z_1(\xi) - z_3(\xi)][z_2(\eta) - z_4(\eta)] + z_1(\xi)[z_3(1) - z_3(0)] \\ &\quad + z_3(\xi)[z_1(0) - z_1(1)] + z_2(\eta)[z_3(1) - z_1(1)] \\ &\quad + z_4(\eta)[z_1(0) - z_3(0)] - D_{\mathrm{II}}. \end{aligned}$$

Proof. It is easy to show that $D_{\mathrm{II}} \to D_{\mathrm{II}} + \zeta E_{\mathrm{II}}$ under the shift operation: merely replace all the elements of $[\tilde{M}]_{ij}$ in (6.26) by $[\tilde{M}]_{ij} + \zeta$ and evaluate $\det(M)$. Similarly, (6.27) may be used to calculate $z(\xi, \eta; \zeta)$, from which z_R is easily obtained. ☐

Figure 6.6 shows z_R on a single region with four different choices of ζ. The possibility of avoiding a folded grid by choosing the right shift makes the method attractive. In addition, many different grids may be obtained on the same region with a minimum of computational effort. This property is useful in testing initial grid dependencies of iterative grid-generation methods. The original grid $z_0(\xi, \eta) = z_R(\xi, \eta; 0)$ is obtained by setting $\zeta = 0$ in (6.124), provided $D_{\mathrm{II}} \neq 0$, as previously noted. If $E_{\mathrm{II}} \neq 0$, a new intrinsic grid formula, the "grid at infinity," $z_\infty(\xi, \eta)$ is obtained from $\lim_{|\zeta| \to \infty} z_R(\xi, \eta; \zeta)$. One finds

$$(6.127) \qquad z_\infty(\xi, \eta) = A(\xi, \eta)/E_{\mathrm{II}}.$$

THEOREM 6.11.2. *The "grid at infinity" is shift invariant.*
The proof is a straightforward computation using (6.126). $z_\infty(\xi, \eta)$ is also invariant under rotation, flip, and stretch. It does not exist when $E_{\mathrm{II}} = 0$. It is also easy to show that $z_\infty(\xi, \eta)$ reduces to the shearing transformation when two opposite sides of Ω are straight lines. Also, applying the boundary-matching condition to (6.127) gives $A(\xi, 0) = z_1(\xi)E_{\mathrm{II}}$, $A(\xi, 1) = z_3(\xi)E_{\mathrm{II}}$, $A(0, \eta) = z_2(\eta)E_{\mathrm{II}}$, and $A(1, \eta) = z_4(\eta)E_{\mathrm{II}}$, showing that $A(\xi, \eta) = 0$ on $\partial\Omega$ if and only if $E_{\mathrm{II}} = 0$.

THEOREM 6.11.3. *The quadrilateral defined by the four corners of the region* Ω *is a parallelogram if and only if* $E_{\mathrm{II}} = 0$.

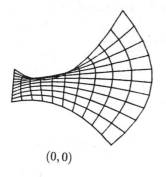

$(0,0)$

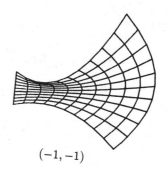

$(-1,-1)$

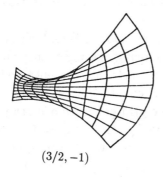

$(3/2,-1)$

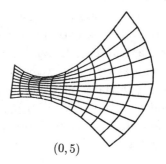

$(0,5)$

FIG. 6.6. *Shifted grids with Alternative* II.

Proof. Suppose $E_{\mathrm{II}} = 0$. Let $w_1 = z_1(1) - z_1(0)$, $w_2 = z_3(0) - z_1(0)$, $w_4 = z_3(1) - z_1(1)$, $w_3 = z_3(1) - z_3(0)$. Then,

$$0 = E_{\mathrm{II}},$$

(6.128)
$$= z_1(0) + z_3(1) - z_1(1) - z_3(0),$$

$$= w_4 - w_2,$$

(6.129)
$$= w_3 - w_1.$$

Hence, $w_4 = w_2$ and $w_3 = w_1$, so that the quadrilateral has opposite sides of equal length. The converse follows immediately. Therefore, the "grid at infinity" exists for all regions Ω, except those that have corners forming a parallelogram. z_∞ is of limited practical value, since many regions of interest possess corners forming a parallelogram. $\square$

THEOREM 6.11.4. *If both $E_{\mathrm{II}} = 0$ and $D_{\mathrm{II}} = 0$, then the quadrilateral formed by the corners of Ω is collapsed to a line, i.e., there are only two distinct corners.*

The proof uses Theorem 6.7.1 and $E_{\mathrm{II}} = 0$ to obtain the result in a straightforward computation. Since no one would want to obtain a grid on such a collapsed region Ω, it is safe to assume that E_{II} and D_{II} are never simultaneously zero for regions of practical interest. There are then three cases:

(i) $D_{\mathrm{II}} \neq 0$ and $E_{\mathrm{II}} \neq 0$. Then

(6.130)
$$z_R(\xi, \eta; \zeta) = \frac{\zeta z_\infty(\xi, \eta) - \zeta_c z_0(\xi, \eta)}{\zeta - \zeta_c},$$

where $\zeta_c = -D_{\mathrm{II}}/E_{\mathrm{II}}$ is referred to as the "critical point" for the grid $z(\xi, \eta)$. Clearly, z_R exists, provided $\zeta \neq \zeta_c$.

(ii) $D_{\mathrm{II}} = 0$ and $E_{\mathrm{II}} \neq 0$. Then

(6.131)
$$z_R(\xi, \eta; \zeta) = z_\infty(\xi, \eta) + \frac{B(\xi, \eta)}{\zeta E_{\mathrm{II}}}.$$

Here it is required that $\zeta \neq 0$ in order for z_R to exist.

(iii) $D_{\mathrm{II}} \neq 0$ and $E_{\mathrm{II}} = 0$. Then

(6.132)
$$z_R(\xi, \eta) = z_0(\xi, \eta) + \frac{\zeta A(\xi, \eta)}{D_{\mathrm{II}}}.$$

Here it is required that $|\zeta| < \infty$ if z_R is to exist.

The expression $D_{\mathrm{II}} + \zeta E_{\mathrm{II}} = E_{\mathrm{II}}(\zeta - \zeta_c)$ is the "shifted denominator" of the restored grid $z_R(\xi, \eta; \zeta)$.

THEOREM 6.11.5. $|D_{\mathrm{II}} + \zeta E_{\mathrm{II}}|$ *is a constant on circles of radius ρ about the critical point ζ_c.*

Proof. Let $\zeta = \zeta_c + \rho e^{i\theta}$, where $0 < \rho < \infty$ and $0 \le \theta < 2\pi$. Then

(6.133)
$$|D_{\mathrm{II}} + \zeta E_{\mathrm{II}}| = |E_{\mathrm{II}} \rho e^{i\theta}|,$$

(6.134)
$$= \rho |E_{\mathrm{II}}|. \qquad \square$$

If $\zeta/(\zeta - \zeta_c)$ is replaced by ζ' in (6.130), the result is $z_R = \zeta' z_\infty + (1 - \zeta')z_0$. This shows that the shift property of the alternative methods is closely related to the idea of the Lagrange interpolation of grids. Let $z_1, z_2, \cdots, z_N$ be N distinct grids on Ω (with $N \geq 2$), and let $\zeta, \zeta_1, \zeta_2, \cdots, \zeta_N \in \mathbf{C}$. Define

$$(6.135) \qquad z(\zeta) = \sum_{n=1}^{N} \left(\prod_{k=1}^{N} \frac{\zeta - \zeta_k}{\zeta_n - \zeta_k} \right) z_n,$$

with $k \neq n$ in the product.

THEOREM 6.11.6. $z(\zeta) \in \mathcal{G}_\Omega$ for all $\zeta \in \mathbf{C}$.

Proof. Let

$$(6.136) \qquad p_n(\zeta) = \prod_{k=1}^{N} \frac{\zeta - \zeta_k}{\zeta_n - \zeta_k}.$$

Then $p_n(\zeta)$ is a polynomial in ζ of degree $N - 1$. Further, $p_n(\zeta_k) = \delta_{nk}$, where δ_{nk} is the Kronecker delta. Let $S(\zeta) = \sum_{n=1}^{N} p_n(\zeta)$; then $S(\zeta)$ is polynomial in ζ of degree less than or equal to $N - 1$. But $S(\zeta_k) = \sum_{n=1}^{N} \delta_{nk} = 1$ for $k = 1, 2, \cdots, N$. Therefore, $S(\zeta) - 1$ is a polynomial of degree at most $N - 1$ having N zeros, $\{\zeta_k\}$. To avoid this contradiction, we must have $S(\zeta) - 1 = 0$ for all ζ. Therefore, on $\partial\Omega$, $z(\zeta) = z_1$, i.e., $z(\zeta)$ matches on the boundary. $\square$

The behavior of Alternative I under a shift is similar to that of Alternative II. The "grid at infinity" in this case may be obtained from (6.126) by replacing z with x and z with y, resulting in the pair $(x_\infty(\xi, \eta), y_\infty(\xi, \eta))$. Alternative III also exhibits similar properties, with grids at infinity possessing over one hundred terms. They are, however, of limited usefulness, since the shifted denominators are zero on parallelograms (and even more general classes of quadrilaterals).

6.12. Grid Control using the Shift Property

The alternative methods under a shift are somewhat limited in their usefulness since (i) they possess critical points in the plane at which they do not exist, (ii) they contain very complicated expressions for the shift parameters involving ratios of polynomials, (iii) the shift property vanishes on regions for which the alternatives reduce to the shearing transformation, and (iv) they cannot be readily extended to higher-dimensional settings. All of these limitations can be avoided using the "cardinality" transfinite interpolation form, while preserving the shift property

$$(6.137) \quad x(\xi, \eta) = g(\eta)x_1(\xi) + f(\eta)x_3(\xi) + k(\xi)x_2(\eta) + h(\xi)x_4(\eta) - e(\xi, \eta),$$

$$(6.138) \quad y(\xi, \eta) = \hat{g}(\eta)y_1(\xi) + \hat{f}(\eta)y_3(\xi) + \hat{k}(\xi)y_2(\eta) + \hat{h}(\xi)y_4(\eta) - \hat{e}(\xi, \eta).$$

$\hat{e}$ is the same as $e(\xi, \eta)$ in (6.106), except with x replaced by y. It is easily shown that the "restored" grid, derived from (6.137) and (6.138) by letting

$x \to x + p$ and $y \to y + q$, is

(6.139) $\quad x^R(\xi, \eta) = x(\xi, \eta) - p(1 - f(\eta) - g(\eta))(1 - h(\xi) - k(\xi))$,

(6.140) $\quad y^R(\xi, \eta) = y(\xi, \eta) - q(1 - \hat{f}(\eta) - \hat{g}(\eta))(1 - \hat{h}(\xi) - \hat{k}(\xi))$.

It is interesting to note that the restored grid in this case is not an interpolation between an unshifted grid and a "grid at infinity," but rather is of the form $x^R = x - pa(\xi, \eta)$, where $a(\xi, \eta)$ is zero on $\partial\Omega$.

The shift property of (6.139) and (6.140) may be exploited by minimizing a functional to obtain an ideal grid within the set of grids generated by all possible shifts. As an example, define the length control functional [19] $F(p, q)$ to be

(6.141)
$$F(p, q) = \sum_{j=2}^{M} \sum_{i=2}^{N+1} \ell_{ij}^2 + \sum_{i=2}^{N} \sum_{j=2}^{M+1} \tilde{\ell}_{ij}^2,$$

where

(6.142) $\quad \ell_{ij}^2 = (x_{ij}^R - x_{i-1,j}^R)^2 + (y_{ij}^R - y_{i-1,j}^R)^2$,

(6.143) $\quad \tilde{\ell}_{ij}^2 = (x_{ij}^R - x_{i,j-1}^R)^2 + (y_{ij}^R - y_{i,j-1}^R)^2$.

It is easy to show that

(6.144) $\quad x_{ij}^R - x_{i-1j}^R = (x_{ij} - x_{i-1j}) + pA_{ij}$,

(6.145) $\quad y_{ij}^R - y_{i-1j}^R = (y_{ij} - y_{i-1j}) + qB_{ij}$,

(6.146) $\quad x_{ij}^R - x_{ij-1}^R = (x_{ij} - x_{ij-1}) + pC_{ij}$,

(6.147) $\quad y_{ij}^R - y_{ij-1}^R = (y_{ij} - y_{ij-1}) + qD_{ij}$,

where

(6.148)
$$A_{ij} = (1 - f(\eta_j) - g(\eta_j))\{(h(\xi_i) - h(\xi_{i-1})) + (k(\xi_i) - k(\xi_{i-1}))\},$$

(6.149)
$$B_{ij} = (1 - \hat{f}(\eta_j) - \hat{g}(\eta_j))\{(\hat{h}(\xi_i) - \hat{h}(\xi_{i-1})) + (\hat{k}(\xi_i) - \hat{k}(\xi_{i-1}))\},$$

(6.150)
$$C_{ij} = (1 - h(\xi_i) - k(\xi_i))\{(f(\eta_j) - f(\eta_{j-1})) + (g(\eta_j) - g(\eta_{j-1}))\},$$

(6.151)
$$D_{ij} = (1 - \hat{h}(\xi_i) - \hat{k}(\xi_i))\{(\hat{f}(\eta_j) - \hat{f}(\eta_{j-1})) + (\hat{g}(\eta_j) - \hat{g}(\eta_{j-1}))\}.$$

Two uncoupled linear equations for p and q are found by setting the gradient to zero:

$$p = -\frac{\sum_{j=2}^{M} \sum_{i=2}^{N+1} A_{ij}(x_{ij} - x_{i-1j}) + \sum_{i=2}^{N} \sum_{j=2}^{M+1} C_{ij}(x_{ij} - x_{ij-1})}{\Lambda_1},$$

$$q = -\frac{\sum_{j=2}^{M} \sum_{i=2}^{N+1} B_{ij}(y_{ij} - y_{i-1j}) + \sum_{i=2}^{N} \sum_{j=2}^{M+1} D_{ij}(y_{ij} - y_{ij-1})}{\Lambda_2},$$

where

$$(6.152) \qquad \Lambda_1 = \sum_{j=2}^{M} \sum_{i=2}^{N+1} A_{ij}^2 + \sum_{i=2}^{N} \sum_{j=2}^{M+1} C_{ij}^2,$$

$$(6.153) \qquad \Lambda_2 = \sum_{j=2}^{M} \sum_{i=2}^{N+1} B_{ij}^2 + \sum_{i=2}^{N} \sum_{j=2}^{M+1} D_{ij}^2.$$

The Hessian is positive definite since

$$(6.154) \qquad H = \begin{pmatrix} \Lambda_1 & 0 \\ 0 & \Lambda_2 \end{pmatrix}.$$

The result is a relatively fast noniterative algorithm that gives the minimum "length" over the space of all grids attainable by the shift. Figure 6.7 shows an example in which the baseline grid generation is the periodic formula (6.107). Other schemes involving different functionals are possible, but the gradient equations are not nearly so simple to solve for the stationary points.

Initial Grid Optimal Grid

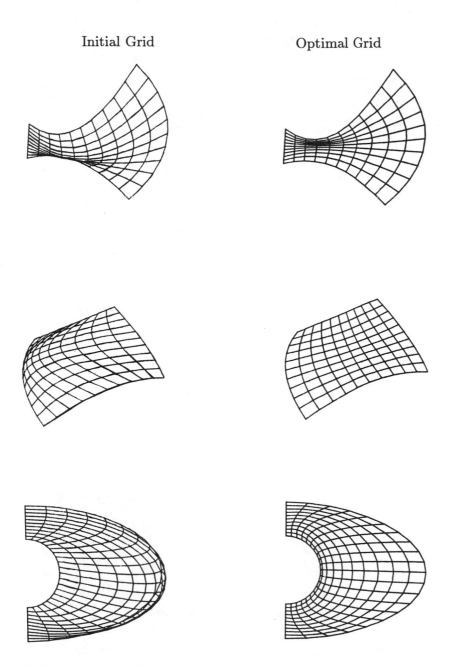

FIG. 6.7. *Algebraic grids resulting from length minimization.*

Initial Grid   "Optimal" Grid

Figure 6.6. Adaptive Grid Generation Prior to Flow Computation

Chapter 7

Surface Grid Generation and Differential Geometry

Z. U. A. Warsi

7.1. Introduction

This paper is aimed at giving a connected account of the selection of model equations for the generation of coordinates in a given surface by using the main results of differential geometry. It is shown that the solution of the proposed model equations satisfies both the equations of Gauss and Weingarten.

The problem of numerical coordinate generation around two-dimensional shapes in planar regions was initiated by Winslow [85] and Chu [21], and later extended to more complicated shapes by Thompson, Thames, and Mastin [74]. The main contribution of [21], [74], and [85] lies in the choice of Laplace/Poisson equations as the grid-generation system. The choice of Laplace equations for the curvilinear coordinate functions in [21], [74], and [85] is based on the simplicity of these equations and, above all, derives from the existence of a maximum principle for such equations. Using the variational principles, Brackbill [12] later showed that the Laplace system yields the smoothest grid system. A comprehensive treatment on the foundation and applications of grid generation in a Euclidean space is available in Thompson, Warsi, and Mastin [75].

The generation of curvilinear coordinates in a curved surface, which forms a two-dimensional non-Euclidean space in a three-dimensional Euclidean space, required a new effort in the choice of a system of partial differential equations. Warsi [81], [80] has proposed a set of elliptic partial differential equations based on some simple differential-geometric concepts and results. The starting point of the work quoted above is that the coordinates in a surface must satisfy the equations or formulas of Gauss. In this paper, and also in [83], the model so obtained has also been shown to be consistent with the equations of Weingarten as well. Some numerical results have been given to demonstrate the applicability of the proposed model equation.

7.2. Basic Equations

The basic partial differential equations of the classic surface theory are available in a number of texts, e.g., Struik [68], Willmore [84], and Kreyszig [44]. Among these equations, the most important are the formulas or equations of Gauss and the equations of Weingarten. Denoting the curvilinear coordinates in a three-dimensional Euclidean space by x^i, $i = 1, 2, 3$, we consider a surface $x^3 = $ const. on which x^α, $\alpha = 1, 2$, are the current curvilinear coordinates. The equations of Gauss in relation to the coordinates considered are

$$(7.1) \qquad \mathbf{r}_{,\alpha\beta} = \Upsilon^\delta_{\alpha\beta}\, \mathbf{r}_{,\delta} + \mathbf{n} b_{\alpha\beta}, \qquad \alpha, \beta = 1, 2\,,$$

while the equations of Weingarten are

$$(7.2) \qquad \mathbf{n}_{,\alpha} = -g^{\beta\gamma} b_{\alpha\beta} \mathbf{r}_{,\gamma}, \qquad \alpha = 1, 2\,,$$

where $\mathbf{r} = (x, y, z)$ with x, y, z as the Cartesian coordinates, and a lower and upper repeated index implies summation. (Note that the Greek indices range over 1 and 2.) In both (7.1) and (7.2), and also in the subsequent analysis, a comma preceding an index in the subscript denotes a partial derivative. Thus,

$$\mathbf{n}_{,\alpha} = \partial \mathbf{n}/\partial x^\alpha\,, \qquad \mathbf{r}_{,\alpha\beta} = \partial^2 \mathbf{r}/\partial x^\alpha \partial x^\beta, \text{ etc.}$$

Further, $\mathbf{n}$ is the unit surface normal vector on the surface $x^3 = $ const.; $g_{\alpha\beta}$ and $b_{\alpha\beta}$ are the coefficients of the first and second fundamental forms, respectively, and $\Upsilon^\delta_{\alpha\beta}$ are the surface Christoffel symbols of the second kind. Thus,

$$(7.3) \qquad \begin{aligned} g_{\alpha\beta} &= \mathbf{r}_{,\alpha} \cdot \mathbf{r}_{,\beta}, \\ b_{\alpha\beta} &= \mathbf{r}_{,\alpha\beta} \cdot \mathbf{n}, \\ \Upsilon^\delta_{\alpha\beta} &= \tfrac{1}{2}\, g^{\sigma\delta} \left(g_{\alpha\sigma,\beta} + g_{\beta\sigma,\alpha} - g_{\alpha\beta,\sigma} \right). \end{aligned}$$

Besides the above-noted equations, it is useful to introduce the second-order differential operator in the surface theory that appears in Beltrami's formulas [68]. This operator is

$$(7.4) \qquad \triangle_2 = \frac{1}{\sqrt{G_3}} \frac{\partial}{\partial x^\alpha} \left(\sqrt{G_3}\, g^{\alpha\beta} \frac{\partial}{\partial x^\beta} \right),$$

where

$$G_3 = g_{11} g_{22} - (g_{12})^2\,, \qquad g^{\alpha\sigma} g_{\beta\sigma} = \delta^\alpha_\beta.$$

The operator in (7.4) is appropriately called the Beltramian operator, although some authors prefer to call it the Laplacian operator.

To establish a clear connection between the development of the model equations for surface coordinate generation and the available classical differential geometric results, we first state a short résumé of some differential geometric results from reference [83]. First of all, the compatibility conditions are obviously

$$(7.5) \qquad \left(\mathbf{r}_{,\alpha\beta} \right)_{,\gamma} = \left(\mathbf{r}_{,\alpha\gamma} \right)_{,\beta}.$$

Using equations (7.1) and (7.2) in equation (7.5), we get

$$(7.6) \qquad b_{\alpha\beta,\gamma} - b_{\alpha\gamma,\beta} = \Upsilon^{\varepsilon}_{\alpha\gamma} \, b_{\varepsilon\beta} - \Upsilon^{\varepsilon}_{\alpha\beta} b_{\varepsilon\gamma},$$

which are two equations: one for $\alpha = 1$, $\beta = 1$, $\gamma = 2$, and the other for $\alpha = 2$, $\beta = 2$, $\gamma = 1$. These equations are known as the Codazzi equations [44]. The other outcome of (7.5) is the Gauss equation

$$(7.7) \qquad R^{\delta}_{\alpha\gamma\beta} = g^{\mu\delta} \left(b_{\alpha\beta} \, b_{\gamma\mu} - b_{\alpha\gamma} \, b_{\beta\mu} \right) ,$$

where

$$R^{\delta}_{\alpha\gamma\beta} = \Upsilon^{\delta}_{\alpha\beta,\gamma} - \Upsilon^{\delta}_{\alpha\gamma,\beta} + \Upsilon^{\varepsilon}_{\alpha\beta}\Upsilon^{\delta}_{\varepsilon\gamma} - \Upsilon^{\varepsilon}_{\alpha\gamma}\Upsilon^{\delta}_{\varepsilon\beta}$$

is the Riemann–Christoffel tensor. From (7.7), four distinct equations can be obtained by taking

$$(7.8) \quad \begin{aligned} \delta = 1: \; &\alpha = 1, \quad \beta = 2, \quad \gamma = 1; \quad \alpha = 2, \quad \beta = 2, \quad \gamma = 1 \\ \delta = 2: \; &\alpha = 1, \quad \beta = 2, \quad \gamma = 1; \quad \alpha = 2, \quad \beta = 2, \quad \gamma = 1. \end{aligned}$$

From the Riemann–Christoffel tensor, the covariant curvature tensor is formed which, in the surface theory, has only one distinct component

$$R_{1212} = b_{11}b_{22} - (b_{12})^2 \; .$$

The Gaussian curvature K is then

$$K = R_{1212} \, / \, G_3 \, .$$

The fundamental theorem of the surface theory is now stated as follows:

If $g_{\alpha\beta}$ and $b_{\alpha\beta}$ are sufficiently differentiable given functions of x^1 and x^2, which satisfy the Gauss–Codazzi equations (7.6) and (7.7) with $G_3 \neq 0$, then there exists a surface which is uniquely determined except for its position in space.

In contrast to the results stated above, the aim of the surface coordinate generation is to generate x, y, z and then to obtain all other geometric quantities $g_{\alpha\beta}$, $b_{\alpha\beta}$, etc., for a *given* surface. Despite the difference in aim, the availability of the equations of differential geometry makes the task of forming the model equations for surface grid generation more systematic and frees one from making a number of unnecessary and arbitrary assumptions. The following subsection deals with the formation of the model equations for surface grid generation.

7.3. Model Equations for Grid Generation

With the aim that a set of partial differential equations be formed from the available equations of differential geometry, we propose to use (7.1) and (7.2) so as to have the Cartesian coordinates as the dependent variables and the curvilinear coordinates as the independent variables. Thus, following [81]–[83], we perform the inner multiplication of (7.1) by $g^{\alpha\beta}$ and obtain

(7.9) $$g^{\alpha\beta}\mathbf{r}_{,\alpha\beta} + \left(\triangle_2 x^\delta\right)\mathbf{r}_{,\delta} = \mathbf{n}\left(k_\mathrm{I} + k_\mathrm{II}\right),$$

where from (7.4),

$$\triangle_2 x^\delta = -g^{\alpha\beta}\Upsilon^\delta_{\alpha\beta}$$

and

$$g^{\alpha\beta}b_{\alpha\beta} = k_\mathrm{I} + k_\mathrm{II}.$$

Here k_I and k_II are the principal curvatures at a point in the surface. Using

$$g^{11} = g_{22}/G_3, \qquad g^{12} = -g_{12}/G_3, \qquad g^{22} = g_{11}/G_3,$$

we can rewrite (7.9) as

(7.10) $$D\mathbf{r} + G_3\left(P\mathbf{r}_\xi + Q\mathbf{r}_\eta\right) = \mathbf{n}R,$$

where $x^1 = \xi$, $x^2 = \eta$, and

$$P = \triangle_2\xi, \qquad Q = \triangle_2\eta,$$
$$D = g_{22}\partial_{\xi\xi} - 2g_{12}\partial_{\xi\eta} + g_{11}\partial_{\eta\eta},$$
$$R = G_3\left(k_\mathrm{I} + k_\mathrm{II}\right) = g_{22}b_{11} - 2g_{12}b_{12} + g_{11}b_{22}.$$

Equation (7.10) provides three scalar equations for the determination of x, y, z when $P = \triangle_2\xi$ and $Q = \triangle_2\eta$ are arbitrarily specified functions. As shown in reference [83], starting from the identity

$$g^{\alpha\beta}\mathbf{r}_{,\beta} = \varepsilon^{\alpha\delta}\mathbf{r}_{,\delta} \times \mathbf{n},$$

where

$$\mathbf{n} = \left(\mathbf{r}_{,1} \times \mathbf{r}_{,2}\right)/\sqrt{G_3},$$
$$\varepsilon^{11} = 0, \qquad \varepsilon^{12} = 1/\sqrt{G_3}, \qquad \varepsilon^{21} = -1/\sqrt{G_3}, \qquad \varepsilon^{22} = 0,$$

and using the Weingarten equations (7.2), one gets

$$\triangle_2\mathbf{r} = b_{\alpha\beta}\,g^{\alpha\beta}\mathbf{n},$$

where $\triangle_2\mathbf{r}$ is the left-hand side of (7.9). From this result, we conclude that the model equation (7.10) satisfies the equations of both Gauss and Weingarten.

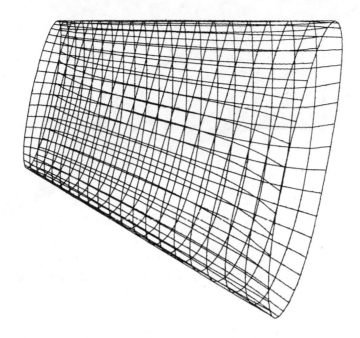

FIG. 7.1. *Coordinates on an elliptic truncated cone:* $x^2/a^2 + y^2/b^2 - (h-z)^2/c^2 = 0$ *from* $z_0 = 0.5\,h$ *to* $z_1 = 0.0; a = 1.0,\ b = 0.5,\ c = 4.0,\ h = 4.0.$

7.4. Numerical Results

Equations (7.10) have been solved by using the point and line SOR techniques for a large number of body shapes [82], [77]. Here, for the purpose of demonstration, we have provided some results for a few geometric shapes (see Figs. 7.1 and 7.2). The differential equations (7.10) need the specification of Dirichlet-type boundary conditions on the boundaries. These equations have also been solved for multiply connected surfaces [82].

From

$$z_0 = 0.5h \quad \text{to} \quad z_1 = 0.0; \qquad \frac{x^2}{a^2} + \frac{y^2}{b^2} - \frac{(h-x)^2}{c^2} = 0,$$
$$a = 1.0, \qquad b = 0.5, \qquad c = 4.0, \qquad h = 4.0,$$

$$z = h\,\mathrm{Sin}\,\frac{\pi x}{a}\,\mathrm{Sin}\frac{\pi y}{b}, \qquad a_1 \le x \le a_2, \qquad b_1 \le y \le b_2,$$
$$a = 1.0, \quad b = 0.5, \quad a_1 = 0, \quad a_2 = 0.5, \quad b_1 = 0, \quad b_2 = 0.5, \quad h = 0.5$$

7.5. Conclusion

This paper develops a set of model equations for the generation of curvilinear coordinate curves in a given surface. It is demonstrated by using the results of differential geometry that any solution of the set of equations (7.10) will simultaneously satisfy the equations of both Gauss and Weingarten.

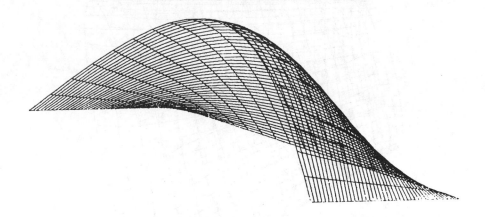

FIG. 7.2. *Coordinates on the surface:* $z = h \, \sin \, (\pi x/a) \, \sin \, (\pi y/b)$, $a_1 \leq x \leq a_2$, $b_1 \leq y \leq b_2; a = 1.0$, $b = 1.0$, $a_1 = 0$, $a_2 = 1.0$, $b_1 = 0$, $b_2 = 0.5$, $h = 0.5$.

7.6. Acknowledgments

This work is an outgrowth of the research supported by the Air Force Office of Scientific Research, through grant AFOSR-85-0143.

Chapter 8

Harmonic Maps in Grid Generation

A. Dvinsky

8.1. Introduction

The grid is an integral part of numerical models constructed using finite-difference and finite-element discretization methods. It is known that the efficiency of numerical discretization methods is enhanced when boundary conditions of modeled problems are applied without interpolation and a regular pattern of connectivity between grid nodes is present. These two requirements are satisfied when the grid is obtained from coordinate transformation such that the boundaries of the considered domain are represented by constant coordinate lines or surfaces. In addition to adapting to the boundaries, the coordinate transformation can be made to adapt to important features of the solution, such as singularities and boundary layers. Such an adaptation is done either prior to solving the numerical problem on the basis of a priori information about the solution or dynamically by adapting to the evolving solution.

Two very successful adaptive grid methods have been built by enhancing the Laplace-equation–based grid generator proposed by Winslow [85] to provide grid control. Thus Godunov and Prokopov [35] proposed to use a system of Poisson equations for grid generation. The left-hand sides of this system were Laplacians operating on curvilinear coordinates, while the right-hand sides contained terms for grid control inside the solution domain. To ensure adequate control over the grid node distribution at the boundaries, the Poisson equations are solved mainly with Dirichlet boundary conditions. The main contribution to further developing and refining the Poisson equation grid generators was made by Thompson and his colleagues. An equidistribution approach by Anderson [3] seems to be the most promising of the solution-adaptive strategies for these grid generators. Although Godunov and Prokopov were able to formulate right-hand sides in such a way that the grid equations satisfied existence and uniqueness conditions, this is not true for arbitrary Poisson equations.

The second method was proposed in the mid-seventies by Yanenko and coworkers (Yanenko, Danaev, and Liseikin [86]; and Liseikin and Yanenko [47]). The authors formulated their approach as a minimization problem, which is probably the most natural framework for building solution-adaptive grid generators. The minimization was carried over a linear combination of several functionals, each measuring a certain property of the coordinate transformation. By manipulating the coefficients in the linear combination, different properties of the resulting mapping are emphasized. It is important to point out that one of the functionals in this system is always the "smoothness" functional, which measures the deviation from the conformal mapping and has as the corresponding Euler–Lagrange equations, Laplacians. Therefore, this approach can be looked at as the extension of the Laplacian-based grid generator.

The Yanenko method has not received as much attention as the Godunov–Thompson method because of its relative complexity. In addition to already cited papers, Brackbill and Saltzman [11] used the above approach to combine the smoothness, orthogonality, and cell size measure functionals to produce the appropriate grid generators. The method has also received attention over the last several years from Castillo and colleagues, who analyzed and further refined this approach (e.g., Castillo [19]). Similar to the Godunov–Thompson grid generators, the existence and uniqueness conditions for most of the grid-generating systems produced using the Yanenko approach are not known.

In this chapter we will present a new method for generating solution-adaptive grids. The method can be thought of as yet another generalization of the basic Laplacian grid generator. However, unlike the two methods discussed above, which in one way or the other *add* terms or functionals to the Laplacian for grid control, the present approach uses a single functional that already contains all the necessary "tools" for grid control. In addition to compactness, the harmonic maps have another important advantage— existence and uniqueness theorems for one-to-one transformations which ensure reliability of grid generators based on harmonic maps.

The rest of this chapter is devoted to the description of solution-adaptive grid generators based on harmonic maps. For additional information, the reader is referred to Dvinsky [25], [26] and to Chapters 9 and 10 in this volume. The following sections provide the necessary background for harmonic maps and formulate sufficient conditions for the existence and uniqueness of harmonic maps (§8.2), discuss and illustrate the concepts presented in the previous section on simple examples (§8.3), formulate adaptive Riemannian metrics (§8.4), show examples of adaptive grids for a convection-diffusion equation (§8.5), and provide the summary (§8.6).

8.2. Harmonic Maps: Definitions and Relevant Theorems

In this section, we introduce harmonic maps and state sufficient conditions for their existence and uniqueness. This subject demands considerably more mathematical presentation than is required elsewhere in this chapter. To make this work more accessible to nonmathematicians, we reiterate and illustrate the main results of this section in §8.3, without the accompanying mathematical rigor.

The theory of harmonic maps is relatively new. Harmonic maps have been defined and named by Fuller [31]. However, until Eells and Sampson's [28] fundamental work, this area of mathematics had not received much study. Since the publication of that paper, harmonic maps have attracted considerable attention from both mathematicians and physicists (e.g., Misner [51]). The development of the theory followed two paths: the study of the existence, uniqueness, and regularity of harmonic maps (e.g., Schoen and Uhlenbeck [58]; Hildebrandt [38]; Jost [41]), and the applications of harmonic maps to different areas in mathematics (see, e.g., the proof of the contractibility of Teichmuller space by Jost [40]). In this work we are primarily concerned with the first path.

Suppose that X and Z are Riemannian manifolds of dimension n with metric tensors $g_{\alpha\beta}$ and G_{ij} in some local coordinates x^n and z^n, respectively. If $x : Z \to X$ is a C^1 map, we define the energy density by

$$(8.1) \qquad e(x) = \frac{1}{2} G^{ij}(z) g_{\alpha\beta}(x) \frac{\partial x^\alpha}{\partial z^i} \frac{\partial x^\beta}{\partial z^j}.$$

Energy associated with the mapping x is then

$$(8.2) \qquad E(x) = \int_Z e(x) dZ.$$

If x is of class C^2, $E(x) < \infty$, and x is a critical point of E, then x is called harmonic. The corresponding Euler equations are given by

$$(8.3) \qquad \frac{1}{\sqrt{G}} \frac{\partial}{\partial z^k} \sqrt{G} G^{kj} \frac{\partial x^\lambda}{\partial z^j} + G^{kj} \Gamma^\lambda_{\alpha\beta} \frac{\partial x^\alpha}{\partial z^k} \frac{\partial x^\beta}{\partial z^j} = 0,$$

where $G = \det(G_{ij})$ and $\Gamma^\lambda_{\alpha\beta}$ are Christoffel symbols of the second kind on x. Thus, we have obtained a system of partial differential equations, where the principal part is a Laplace–Beltrami operator, while the nonlinearity is quadratic in the gradient of solution.

Next, we formulate sufficient conditions for the existence and uniqueness of harmonic maps. The theorem shown, referred to here as the HSY theorem, is due to Hamilton [36] and Schoen and Yau [57].

THEOREM 8.2.1 (Hamilton–Schoen–Yau (HSY)). *Let (X,ρ), (Z,ν) be two Riemannian manifolds with boundaries ∂X and ∂Z, and $\phi : X \to Z$ be a diffeomorphism. For any map $f : X \to Z$ such that $f_{|\partial X} = \phi_{|\partial X}$, we define $E(f) = \int_X \| df \|^2 dX$. We say that f is harmonic if it is an extremal of E.*

THEOREM 8.2.2. *If the curvature of Z is nonpositive, and ∂Z is convex (with respect to metric ν), then there exists a unique harmonic map $f : X \to Z$ such that f is a homotopy equivalent to ϕ. (In other words, f can be deformed to ϕ.)*

The HSY theorem is valid for n-dimensional, multiconnected domains. For certain choices of metrics in the mapped domains, the theorem reduces to the maximum principle for linear elliptic partial differential equations (e.g., Birkhoff and Lynch [9]).

8.3. Application of the HSY Theorem

The HSY theorem states sufficient conditions for the existence and uniqueness of harmonic maps—solutions to (8.3). Suppose X is a given physical domain and Z is a constructed (computational or logical) domain. Then according to the theorem, a harmonic $Z \to X$ map exists and is one-to-one when the following two conditions are satisfied:

    1. The curvature of X is nonpositive, and

    2. ∂X is convex.

The first condition can be readily satisfied by defining an appropriate metric, for example, Euclidean, on X. (The Euclidean space is "flat," i.e., it has zero curvature.) If, in addition, the boundary of the physical domain is convex, the $Z \to X$ mapping can always be accomplished.

    The equation used to accomplish $X \to Z$ harmonic mapping is given by

$$(8.4) \qquad \frac{1}{\sqrt{g}} \frac{\partial}{\partial x^k} \sqrt{g} g^{kj} \frac{\partial z^\lambda}{\partial x^j} + g^{kj} \Gamma^\lambda_{\alpha\beta} \frac{\partial z^\alpha}{\partial x^k} \frac{\partial z^\beta}{\partial x^j} = 0,$$

where $g = \det(g_{ij})$ and $\Gamma^\lambda_{\alpha\beta}$ are Christoffel symbols of the second kind on z. This mapping is guaranteed to exist and to be unique when the computational domain Z has both the nonpositive curvature and the convex boundary. Since Z is obtained by construction, both requirements can always be met. Therefore, in general, it is better to use an $X \to Z$ map, since in such a case a diffeomorphism is assured under conditions of the HSY theorem. The disadvantage of the latter mapping is that it requires one to solve the inverse of (8.4), which is significantly more complex than (8.3).

    The following two examples illustrate the above discussion regarding the direction of mapping. Consider (8.3) for mapping between two Euclidean domains, that is, $g_{ij} = G_{ij} = \delta_{ij}$, where δ_{ij} is the Kronecker delta:

$$(8.5) \qquad\qquad\qquad x_{\xi\xi} + x_{\eta\eta} = 0,$$

$$(8.6) \qquad\qquad\qquad y_{\xi\xi} + y_{\eta\eta} = 0,$$

where $(x, y) \in X$ and $(\xi, \eta) \in Z$. The map shown is $Z \to X$ and hence, to satisfy the HSY theorem, X has to have a nonpositive curvature and ∂X must be convex. The first condition is satisfied because we set $g_{ij} = \delta_{ij}$, which implies zero curvature. Then, if ∂X is convex we will be able to obtain a grid independently of the shape of ∂Z. It can be shown that, if equations (8.5) and (8.6) are discretized using central differences, the above statement is valid for any grid density, since the discretized equations satisfy the maximum principle. Suppose we map domain Z, shown in Fig. 8.1(a), onto a unit square, domain

X. The resulting grid is shown in Fig. 8.2. If, however, ∂X is not convex (as is the case for domain Z shown in Fig. 8.1(a)), a solution to equations (8.5) and (8.6) may not exist. In fact, such a mapping was attempted by Amsden and Hirt [2], who mapped a square logical domain onto a domain similar to the one shown in Fig. 8.1(a). In their calculation, the grid folded as it did in our calculation, shown in Fig. 8.3.

Consider now a harmonic map in the opposite direction, $X \to Z$, which is given by a solution to (8.4). As in the previous example, assume a Euclidean metric in both domains. The resulting system is the same as the one originally proposed by Winslow [85]:

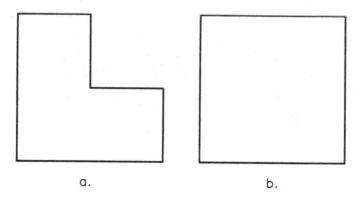

a.   b.

FIG.   8.1.   *Examples of domains with a concave boundary* (a) *and a convex boundary* (b).

$$(8.7) \qquad\qquad \xi_{xx} + \xi_{yy} = 0,$$

$$(8.8) \qquad\qquad \eta_{xx} + \eta_{yy} = 0.$$

A map by (8.7), (8.8) exists and is a diffeomorphism for convex ∂Z. The usual way to solve this map is, however, to transform it to the logical space variables.   The transformation yields the following quasi-linear system of equations (Thompson, Warsi, and Mastin [75]):

$$(8.9) \qquad\qquad g_{22}x_{\xi\xi} - 2g_{12}x_{\xi\eta} + g_{11}x_{\eta\eta} = 0,$$

$$(8.10) \qquad\qquad g_{22}y_{\xi\xi} - 2g_{12}y_{\xi\eta} + g_{11}y_{\eta\eta} = 0,$$

where $g_{22} = x_\eta^2 + y_\eta^2$, $g_{11} = x_\xi^2 + y_\xi^2$, and $g_{12} = x_\xi x_\eta + y_\xi y_\eta$. Although the solution of (8.9), (8.10) must be the same as that for (8.7), (8.8), and hence must be a diffeomorphism, it is not obvious that any consistent finite-difference form of (8.9), (8.10) produces a diffeomorphism for any grid density. Our experience, however, has shown that (8.9), (8.10) is indeed very robust for a wide variety of problems.

Here we would like to mention just one peculiar example of using (8.7), (8.8) and (8.9), (8.10); a detailed discussion of this case can be found in Dvinsky

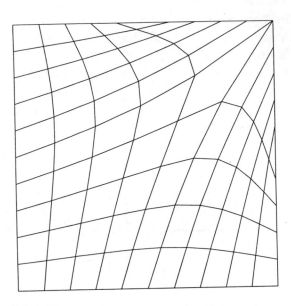

FIG. 8.2. *Mapping of domain shown in Fig. 8.1(a) onto domain in Fig 8.1(b) using equations (8.5) and (8.6).*

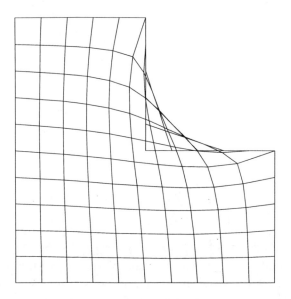

FIG. 8.3. *Mapping of domain shown in Fig. 8.1(b) onto domain in Fig. 8.1(a) using equations (8.5) and (8.6).*

[26]. Consider a map of a square physical domain onto a computational domain shown in Fig. 8.1(a) using (8.7), (8.8). Except for notation, this is exactly the same problem we calculated above using (8.5), (8.6); this problem did not have a solution. By solving (8.9), (8.10), however, we obtain a one-to-one map.

A few words now about the numerical solution of (8.3). This equation is discretized using second-order central differences for second derivatives. Using the second-order central differences for approximation of the first derivative, however, causes the appearance of oscillating modes for high values of $G^{kj}\Gamma^{\lambda}_{\alpha\beta}$. One way to eliminate these modes is to use one-sided (upwind) first-order accurate differences for the first derivatives. But accuracy of this approximation is often not sufficient, especially for two- and three-dimensional problems where one is often forced to use rather coarse grids. (We assume that (8.3) describes a nearly optimal coordinate transformation and hence its accurate solution *is* important.) A simple remedy in this case is to use a product of forward and backward one-sided first-order accurate differences, for example, in one dimension, $x_z^2 \approx (x_{i+1} - x_i)(x_i - x_{i-1})$. The resulting approximation of the nonlinear term is then second-order accurate.

We tried several different approaches to linearize (8.3). The Picard linearization, when the nonlinear terms are calculated explicitly (e.g., Ames [1]), does not work for large values of $G^{kj}\Gamma^{\lambda}_{\alpha\beta}$. We also tried

$$\frac{1}{\sqrt{G}}\frac{\partial}{\partial z^k}\sqrt{G}G^{kj}\frac{\partial x^{\lambda,n+1}}{\partial z^j} + G^{kj}\Gamma^{\lambda}_{\alpha\beta}\frac{\partial x^{\alpha,n+1}}{\partial z^k}\frac{\partial x^{\beta,n}}{\partial z^j} = 0,$$

where n is the iteration level, and the Newton linearization

$$\frac{1}{\sqrt{G}}\frac{\partial}{\partial z^k}\sqrt{G}G^{kj}\frac{\partial x^{\lambda,n+1}}{\partial z^j} + 2G^{kj}\Gamma^{\lambda}_{\alpha\beta}\frac{\partial x^{\alpha,n+1}}{\partial z^k}\frac{\partial x^{\beta,n}}{\partial z^j} - G^{kj}\Gamma^{\lambda}_{\alpha\beta}\frac{\partial x^{\alpha,n}}{\partial z^k}\frac{\partial x^{\beta,n}}{\partial z^j} = 0.$$

Both of these procedures worked well in our tests for any value of $G^{kj}\Gamma^{\lambda}_{\alpha\beta}$.

8.4. Formulation of Riemannian Metrics

To be able to use harmonic maps for solution-adaptive grid generation, one has to formulate an expression for Riemannian metrics in the mapped manifolds. For the convenience of discussion, we will differentiate between two types of adaptation: geometrical and physical. We term geometrical adaptation as the process in which the grid clusters in specified (fixed) geometric locations. The physical adaptation is defined as the usual solution-adaptive process in which the grid is adaptively modified in response to evolving physical solution.

We will consider geometrical adaptation first because it is somewhat conceptually simpler than the physical one, while at the same time it will enable us to introduce all the necessary elements for the physical adaptation. We will start with a simple quasi–one-dimensional problem, where we will try to generate a grid clustered around a straight vertical line midway in a square physical domain X. We will use an $X \rightarrow Z$ mapping. The logical domain, denoted by Z, is, for this problem, a rectangle, the size of which is determined by the number of grid nodes selected in respective directions. First, we want to make sure that the curvature of the logical domain is nonpositive by defining $G_{ij} = \delta_{ij}$.

The next step is to define the physical space metrics g_{ij}. To provide a higher resolution, the metrics should increase in specified locations and revert to their original state away from these regions. In addition, we want the metric to adapt to the shape of the attraction lines, which in this example is just a straight vertical line. Such a metric can be written as

$$(8.11) \qquad g_{11} = 1 + f(x - x_o),$$

$$(8.12) \qquad g_{22} = 1, \qquad g_{12} = 0,$$

where $x = x_o$ is the selected line of attraction and $f(x - x_o)$ is defined to have a maximum when $x = x_o$ and $f(x - x_o) \to 0$ as $(x - x_o) \to \infty$. An example of such a function is given by

$$(8.13) \qquad f(x - x_o) = Ae^{-B(x-x_o)^2},$$

where A and B are positive constants controlling the amplitude and the rate of decay of $f(.)$.

A two-dimensional example is provided by attraction to a circle in the physical domain. Consider a rectangular physical domain and a circle of radius R with its center at (x_c, y_c), so that the entire circle is inside the domain. We want to construct a Riemannian metric that would expand at the rim of the circle and decay to the standard Euclidean metric as the distance from the rim increases. Noting that a circle is a straight line in polar coordinates, we can immediately write the expression for the metric using the results of the previous example:

$$(8.14) \qquad g_{11} = \frac{f(\rho - R)(x - x_c)^2 + (y - y_c)^2}{\rho^2},$$

$$(8.15) \qquad g_{22} = \frac{(x - x_c)^2 + f(\rho - R)(y - y_c)^2}{\rho^2},$$

$$(8.16) \qquad g_{12} = \frac{(x - x_c)(y - y_c)(f(\rho - R) - 1)}{\rho^2},$$

where $\rho^2 = (x - x_c)^2 + (y - y_c)^2$ and R is the radius of the circle.

These results can be generalized for attraction to an arbitrary curve, point, or any combination thereof. Suppose that the attraction locations are given by function $F(x) = 0$, $\{x\} = \{x^1, x^2, x^3\}$. It then follows that

$$(8.17) \qquad g_{ij} = \delta_{ij} + f(F)\frac{F_{x^i} F_{x^j}}{(\nabla F)^2},$$

where $f(F)$ is a function of the distance from a given point to $F(x) = 0$ such that $f(F)$ increases as the distance tends to zero and goes to zero as the distance increases, and the subscript denotes the partial derivative with respect to x^i. Thus, the adaptive Riemannian metric consists of the Euclidean δ_{ij} and a non-Euclidean part, $f(F)(F_{x^i}F_{x^j}/(\nabla F)^2)$. The non-Euclidean part is in turn a product of the magnification factor, $f(F)$, which controls the magnitude of the metrics and the directional factor, $F_{x^i}F_{x^j}/(\nabla F)^2$, which modifies the magnitude, depending on the direction of selected contour lines.

Equation (8.17) requires calculation of the shortest distance from each grid node x_o to $F(x) = 0$, which is computationally expensive. This calculation, however, can be readily eliminated if we notice that $F(x_o)$ is a measure of distance from x_o to $F(x)$. Incidentally, in both previous examples, $F(x_o)$ is exactly the shortest distance between x_o and $F(x)$.

Using the above modification to (8.17), we calculated an example of a grid attracted to two intersecting straight lines, $y = x$ and $y = -x + 1$, so that $F = (y - x)(y + x - 1)$. The grid shown in Fig. 8.4 was calculated from equation (8.4), with g_{ij} from (8.17), $G_{ij} = \delta_{ij}$, and $f(F) = F(x, y)$.

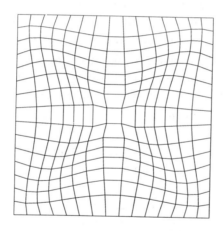

FIG. 8.4. *A grid adapted to two intersecting lines, $y = x$ and $y = -x + 1$.*

The procedure for the geometric adaptation described above can be readily extended to the physical adaptation. Suppose one can formulate a scalar function that characterizes and monitors the essential features of the physical problem. Fortunately, this often can be accomplished, since the evolving solution is usually controlled by just a few critical variables. These variables, or some suitable function of them, can then be combined into a single scalar function, the characteristic function. Recall that the expression for Riemannian metrics (8.17) adapts the metrics to the contours of the continuously or discretely specified scalar function $F(x)$. Therefore, once the characteristic function is defined, the physical metrics are given   by the same expression as the geometric ones. Examples of the physical adaptation are shown in the next section.

8.5. Numerical Examples

In this section we show how to apply the concepts presented above to the numerical solution of the convection-diffusion equation

$$(8.18) \qquad Ru_x = u_{xx} + u_{yy} + \alpha^2(1 - e^{R(x-1)})\sin\alpha y,$$

with the exact solution given by

$$(8.19) \qquad u = (1 - e^{R(x-1)})\sin\alpha y,$$

where R and α are parameters. The solution of (8.18) is first calculated on a unit square with a uniform mesh. Once the solution is obtained, we use it to define a characteristic function, which is, in turn, employed to form a Riemannian metric in the physical space. Next, the adaptive grid is obtained from harmonic maps. Equation (8.18) is then solved on the adapted grid, and its solution is compared with the solution obtained on the uniform grid.

Equation (8.18) is solved as follows. First, it is transformed to curvilinear coordinates and then discretized using central differences for second-order derivatives and first-order upwind differences for first-order derivatives. The resulting difference equations are solved using the Red-Black Successive Overrelaxation (SOR) method with Chebyshev acceleration to machine accuracy (6–7 digits on our 32-bit machine).

We use (8.4) to calculate the coordinate transformation. To assure the nonpositive curvature on Z, the metric in the computational domain is assumed to be Euclidean. As a result, the nonlinear terms in (8.4) vanish identically to yield

$$(8.20) \qquad \frac{1}{\sqrt{g}}\frac{\partial}{\partial x^k}\sqrt{g}g^{kj}\frac{\partial z^\lambda}{\partial x^j} = 0.$$

Equation (8.20) is inverted to computational coordinates and discretized using central differences both for the first- and second-order derivatives.

During the adaptive grid calculation, as the grid moves away from its initial position, the characteristic function is no longer available at the new locations. To obtain the characteristic function at these locations, one either has to recalculate the physical problem, in our case solve (8.18), or interpolate the characteristic function after each iteration on grid equations to new grid locations. Both procedures in the "real-life problems" are quite expensive. Nevertheless, to demonstrate the potential of the method, we calculate both examples in a coupled fashion. The coupling, however, is effected in a "quasi-coupled" fashion (see below), where the grid is calculated to full convergence for each F field until the next iteration is started. Such a procedure allows one to clearly see the effects of coupling on the solution.

In the first example, we used the Dirichlet boundary conditions in an effort to maintain consistency with the HSY theorem. For example, $y = 0$ and

$x = (i-1)/(I_{\max} - 1)$, where $i = 1, 2 \cdots$. The parameters in (8.18) were set to $R = 10$ and $\alpha = \pi$. The numerical solution calculated on the uniform Cartesian 12×12 grid is shown in Fig. 8.5 and the error E, $E \equiv (|\, [u]_{ij} - u_{ij} \,|)/(1 - e^{-R})$, is shown in Fig. 8.6. $[u]_{ij}$ and u_{ij} are the analytical and numerical solutions at the grid node (i, j), respectively. Although we used 11 contours in all figures, sometimes fewer than 11 contours are visible, which indicates that maximum and/or minimum coincides with the boundary or the maximum and/or minimum contour is just a single point.

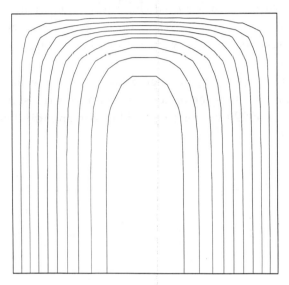

FIG. 8.5.   *Contours of u calculated from equation* (8.18).

FIG. 8.6. *Contours of E after the first iteration. E = 0 at the boundary and* $E_{\max}$ *is at* $(x, y) = (0.85, 0.33)$.

The maximum error and the average error per grid node for the solution calculated on the uniform grid are $E_{\max} = 0.103$ and $E_{av} = 0.00367$, respectively. In this example, the characteristic function is defined to be the numerical solution itself, that is, $F_{ij} \equiv u_{ij}$, while function $f(F)$, from (8.17), is defined as $f(F) = 1 + (\nabla F/\nabla F_{av})$. We adopted the following procedure to obtain the adaptive grid:

1. Solve (8.18) to roundoff;
2. Calculate the grid from (8.20), also solved to roundoff;
3. Repeat steps (1) and (2).

As we stated earlier, we followed this rather inefficient procedure instead of employing a solution that was either simultaneous or sequential, with just a few inner iterations, because we wanted to show the effect of coupling on the resulting solution.

The first iteration of the above algorithm yields the grid shown in Fig. 8.7. The maximum and average error for the adapted grid solution are $E_{\max} = 0.0557$ and $E_{av} = 0.00229$, respectively. The corresponding error contours are shown in Fig. 8.8.

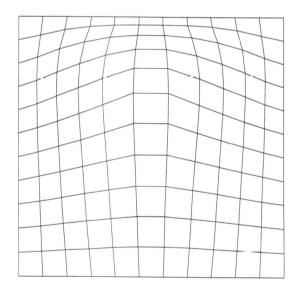

FIG. 8.7.   *The adapted grid after the first iteration.*

The maximum and average errors for the second iteration were $E_{\max} = 0.0447$ and $E_{av} = 0.00186$; for the third, $E_{\max} = 0.0400$ and $E_{av} = 0.00165$; and for the fourth, $E_{\max} = 0.0369$ and $E_{av} = 0.00155$, respectively. The grid calculated in the fourth iteration (i.e., the one based on the solution from the third iteration) is shown in Fig. 8.9. The error contours for the fourth iteration are shown in Fig. 8.10.

As the iteration continues, the grid becomes more skewed. Thus the average angle after the first iteration is 78°, with 85 percent of the angles being greater than 67.5°; while after the fourth iteration the average angle

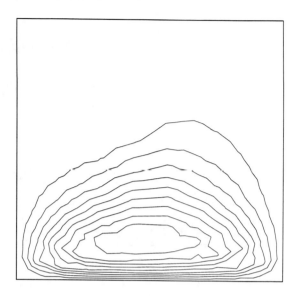

FIG. 8.8. *Contours of E calculated on the grid shown in Fig 8.7. $E_{\max}$ is at* $(x, y) = (0.84, 0.44)$.

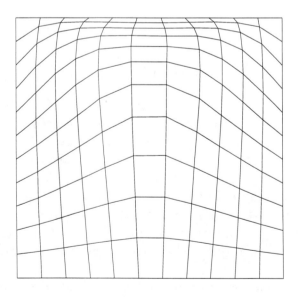

FIG. 8.9. *The adapted grid after the fourth iteration.*

FIG. 8.10. *Contours of E calculated on the grid shown in Fig. 8.9. $E_{\max}$ is at $(x, y) = (0.83, 0.57)$.*

drops to 66°, with 7 percent of the angles being less than 45° and 44 percent of the angles measuring between 45° and 67.5°.

In the second example, we use the following boundary conditions for the grid equations (8.20):

$$x^1(1, z^2) = 0 \quad \text{and} \quad \partial x^2/\partial z^1_{|x^1=0} = 0; \qquad x^1(z^1_{\max}, z^2) = 0$$

and

$$\partial x^2/\partial z^1_{|x^1=1} = 0; \qquad x^2(z^1, 1) = 0 \quad \text{and} \quad \partial x^1/\partial z^2_{|x^2=0} = 0;$$

and finally $x^2(z^1, z^2_{\max}) = 1$ and $\partial x^1/\partial z^2_{|x^2=1} = 0$, where for all $x^i \in [0, 1]$ and for all $z^i \in [1, z^i_{\max}]$. Since Neumann conditions are used, the HSY theorem no longer applies to this mapping. The effect of using the Neumann condition, if the mapping exists at all, will be to reduce the grid skewing and hence, possibly, to improve the solution accuracy. The boundary conditions for the grid equations is the only difference between this and the previous example.

The grid obtained after the first iteration is shown in Fig. 8.11. The maximum and average errors for the adapted grid solution are $E_{\max} = 0.0589$ and $E_{\text{av}} = 0.00231$, respectively. The corresponding error contours are shown in Fig. 8.12.

The maximum and average error, for the second iteration were $E_{\max} = 0.0445$ and $E_{\text{av}} = 0.00172$; for the third, $E_{\max} = 0.0416$ and $E_{\text{av}} = 0.00151$; and for the fourth, $E_{\max} = 0.0391$ and $E_{\text{av}} = 0.00141$, respectively. The grid calculated in the fourth iteration (i.e., the one based on the solution from the third iteration) is shown in Fig. 8.13. The error contours for the fourth iteration are shown in Fig. 8.14.

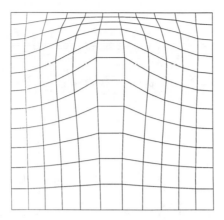

FIG. 8.11. *The adapted grid calculated with Neumann boundary conditions after the first iteration.*

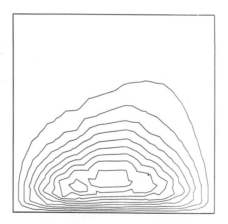

FIG. 8.12. *Contours of E calculated on the grid shown in Fig 8.11. $E_{\max}$ is at $(x, y) = (0.88, 0.33)$.*

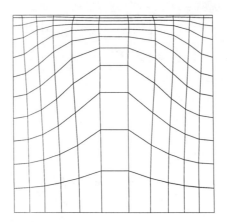

FIG. 8.13. *The adapted grid calculated with Neumann boundary conditions after the fourth iteration.*

FIG. 8.14. *Contours of E calculated on the grid shown in Fig 8.13. $E_{\max}$ is at $(x, y) = (0.74, 0.57)$.*

As expected, the grid in this simulation is less skewed than the grid in the first one. Thus, the average angle after the first iteration is 78°, with 83 percent of the angles being greater than 67.5°; and after the fourth iteration the average angle is 76°, with 21 percent of the angles measuring between 45° and 67.5°, and the rest measuring greater than 67.5°. The somewhat unexpected result is that the improved grid properties have not improved the numerical solution.

The examples presented in this section illustrate how the concepts shown in this work can be applied to generating adaptive grids for a model diffusion-convection equation. Using a simple, common-sense formulation for the characteristic function, we have obtained grids that have helped to reduce the error in the maximum norm by almost a factor of three. It is also notable that we have not used any adjustable parameters in the definition of the metrics. We believe that still better results could be achieved, provided there exists an optimal formulation for the characteristic function. Developing general guidelines and rules for such a formulation, possibly just for certain classes of the partial differential equation, will be the subject of future research.

8.6. Conclusions

In this chapter, we described a new framework for adaptive grid generation based on the principles of differential geometry. In particular, we have utilized an apparatus of harmonic maps for our construction. The described method has several attractive features, such as compactness of the governing equations, clarity of formulation, and reliability. The feasibility and effectiveness of the proposed approach were established by formulating adaptive Riemannian metrics in mapped domains and actually performing the numerical mapping. In addition, we investigated the question of the existence and uniqueness of harmonic maps and formulated sufficient conditions for our application using results by Hamilton [36] and Schoen and Yau [57].

8.7. Acknowledgments

The author thanks Professor David Kazhdan of Harvard University for many useful discussions and suggestions during this work. The author would also like to thank Jacqueline Temple for her efforts in the preparation of this manuscript. This research has been sponsored by National Science Foundation grant ISI 8660378.

Chapter 9

On Harmonic Maps

G. Liao

9.1. Introduction

Harmonic maps between Riemannian manifolds Ω and $\bar{\Omega}$ are critical points of the energy functional. In the special case, when both Ω and $\bar{\Omega}$ are domains in Euclidean space, a harmonic map φ from Ω into $\bar{\Omega}$ satisfies the Laplace equation $\triangle \varphi = 0$. In the general case, when Ω and $\bar{\Omega}$ are equipped with Riemannian metrics g and $\bar{g}$, respectively, the harmonic map equation is a semilinear elliptic system, which will be derived in §9.3.

In the case $n = \dim \Omega = \dim \bar{\Omega} = 2$, harmonic maps (and solutions to Poisson equation $\triangle \varphi = f$) have been successfully used to generate grids in computational problems (see [76], [4]).

Let $\varphi : \Omega \to \bar{\Omega}$ be a mapping, where $\Omega \subset \mathbb{R}^n$ is a bounded domain (the physical domain),

$$\bar{\Omega} = [a_1, b_1] \times \cdots \times [a_n, b_n]$$

(the computational domain). To generate grids in $\bar{\Omega}$, one approach is to solve $\triangle \varphi = 0$ subject to the boundary condition that φ restricted to $\partial \Omega$ is a prescribed homeomorphism from $\partial \Omega$ to $\partial \bar{\Omega}$. The maximum principle of the Laplace equation (and elliptic equations in general) guarantees that the image of Ω by φ will be contained in $\bar{\Omega}$, since the image of $\partial \Omega$ is contained in $\partial \bar{\Omega}$. The main mathematical problem here is to make φ a diffeomorphism, i.e., the one-to-one, onto, and Jacobian conditions of φ do not vanish.

In the case where $n = 2$, the mathematical foundation of this approach is solid. We have Theorem 9.1.1, which is due to Rado [55].

THEOREM 9.1.1. *Let Ω and $\bar{\Omega}$ be simply connected bounded domains in $\mathbb{R}^2$. Let $\bar{\Omega}$ be convex. Let $\varphi : \Omega \to \bar{\Omega}$ be a harmonic map such that $\varphi : \partial \Omega \to \partial \bar{\Omega}$ is a homeomorphism. Then, the Jacobian of φ does not vanish in the interior of Ω.*

Remark. From this it follows that, in fact, φ is one-to-one and onto, and hence, a diffeomorphism. For a proof of this, one can see Theorem 2 of [50].

Rado's theorem can be proved by the following steps (see, e.g., [48]):

Step 1. Introduce the coordinates $(x, y) \in \Omega$ and $(u, v) \in \bar{\Omega}$ (see

Fig. 9.1). Assume that $J = (D(u,v))/(D(x,y)) = 0$ at an interior point $P_o = (x_o, y_o) \in \Omega$. Then there exists c_1 and $c_2 \in \mathbb{R}^1$ such that at P_o

$$c_1 u_x + c_2 v_x = 0,$$
$$c_1 u_y + c_2 v_y = 0.$$

Let $h = c_1 u + c_2 v$. Then $\triangle h = 0$ and

$$\nabla h(P_o) = c_1 \nabla u(P_o) + c_2 \nabla v(P_o) = 0,$$

where

$$\nabla u = (u_x, u_y), \qquad \nabla v = (v_x, v_y).$$

Step 2. Expanding h at $P = P_o$ in terms of spherical harmonics, we get

$$h(P) = h(P_o) + S_2 + S_3 + \cdots,$$

where S_k is a kth-order homogeneous harmonic polynomial. The linear term is missing because $\nabla h(P_o) = 0$.

Step 3. It follows that the level set $L = \{P \in \Omega \mid h(P) = h(P_o)\}$ has at least four branches joining at P_o. In fact, by Courant's nodal line theorem, these branches form an equiangular system of rays at P_o (see Fig. 9.2).

Step 4. These rays cannot close off in the interior of D. Otherwise, h must be constant according to the maximum principle. This would imply that the image of ∂D by φ is contained in a straight line $c_1 u + c_2 v = h(P_o)$, a contradiction. Thus, these rays must go all the way to the boundary ∂D, and $L \cap \partial D$ contains at least four points (see Fig. 9.3).

Step 5. Since a straight line intersects the boundary $\partial \bar{D}$ of a convex domain $\bar{D}$ at no more than two points, we get a contradiction: at least four points of ∂D are mapped by φ to two points of $\partial \bar{D}$ (see Fig. 9.3).

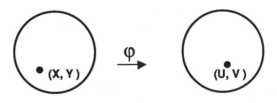

FIG. 9.1

In the case where $n \geq 3$, the problem becomes much more involved. The analogue of Rado's theorem is not known. The main purpose of this article is to analyze the three-dimensional geometry and to identify some of the difficulties that stay in the way of applying harmonic maps in three-dimensional grid generation. In particular, we will point out that for $n = 3$, Step 3 is unclear, and Step 4 is not true. Our main reference is a paper by Lewy [45], who constructed explicit examples of nonconstant harmonic functions

FIG. 9.2

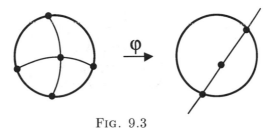

FIG. 9.3

$h = \mathbb{R}^3 \to \mathbb{R}^1$, whose level set $L = \{P \in \partial B^3 | h = 0\}$ divides ∂B^3 into exactly two components. Thus, even Rado's theorem may still be true for $n = 3$, the straightforward extension of its proof, which is outlined above (see also [50]), is false.

9.2. Hans Lewy's Example

Next, we will outline the construction of a class of harmonic functions with the stated property. We begin with some terminology.

DEFINITION. A real-valued function $h(x, y, z)$ is called a *spherical harmonic* of degree k if h is a polynomial of degree k such that

$$\triangle h = h_{xx} + h_{yy} + h_{zz} = 0$$

and

$$h(\lambda x, \lambda y, \lambda z) = \lambda^k h(x, y, z), \quad \forall \lambda \in \mathbb{R}^1.$$

DEFINITION. The set $\{(x, y, z) \in \mathbb{R}^3 \,|\, x^2 + y^2 + z^2 = 1,\ h(x, y, z) = 0\}$ is called *nodal lines* of h.

Lewy's main idea is to perturb the harmonic function $\mathrm{Im}(x + i\,y)^k$ on the xy-plane, whose nodal lines are straight lines through the origin. The x-axis is one of them. Any two adjacent nodal lines form an equal angle $\pi/4$ (see Fig. 9.4).

In $\mathbb{R}^3$, using the homogeneity allows one to write that, for $z \neq 0, h(x, y, z) = z^k h\,(x/z,\ y/z,\ 1)$. Thus, the study of nodal lines can be reduced to a two-variable problem. Let $N = $ the North Pole $ = (0, 0, 1); S = $ the South Pole $ = (0, 0, -1)$. Then, the nodal lines of $\mathrm{Im}\,(x + iy)^k$ on S^2 are great circles going through N and S, forming an equal angle π/k (see Fig. 9.5).

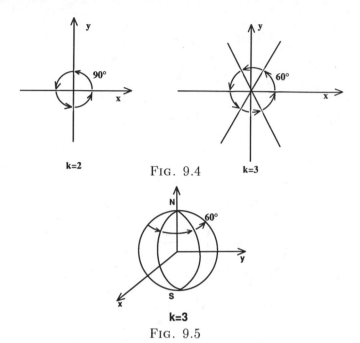

FIG. 9.4

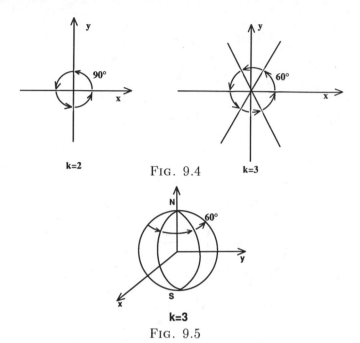

FIG. 9.5

Now, a small perturbation $-\epsilon f(x, y, z)$ is added to $\text{Im}(x + iy)^k$, where f is a spherical harmonic of degree k with $f(0, 0, 1) > 0$. Let $h = \text{Im} (x + iy)^k - \epsilon f(x, y, z)$. There are several cases:

(1) Near N, we have $\epsilon f(x, y, z) = \epsilon z^k f(x/z, y/z, 1) > 0$. For x and y small, $z \approx 1$, it can be proved that nodal lines of h, when viewed from the z direction, look like the array displayed in Fig. 9.6.

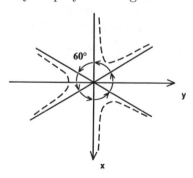

FIG. 9.6

(2) Near S, if $k = $ odd, then $\epsilon f(x, y, z) = \epsilon z^k (x/z, y/z, 1) < 0$. The nodal lines for x, y small and $z \approx -1$ are shown in Fig. 9.7 (again viewed from the z direction).

(3) Away from N and S, the nodal lines of h are small perturbations of great circles that form the nodal lines of $\text{Im } (x + iy)^k$ (see Fig. 9.8).

Thus, we are led to the following theorem.

THEOREM 9.2.1 (Lewy). *Let $k = $ odd. There exists a spherical harmonic h of degree k whose nodal lines divide the unit sphere into exactly two components*

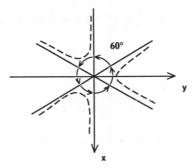

FIG. 9.7

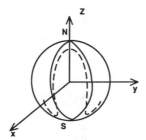

FIG. 9.8

in which $h \neq 0$. In fact, for small $\epsilon > 0$, $h(x, y, z) = \mathrm{Im}(x - i\,y)^k - \epsilon f(x, y, z)$, with f a spherical harmonic of degree k such that $f(0, 0, 1) > 0$ has the required property.

A concrete example is

$$h = 3\,x^2\,y - y^3 - \epsilon\,(2\,z^3 - 3\,x^2\,z - 3\,y^2\,z), \quad \text{where } \epsilon > 0 \text{ is sufficiently small.}$$

Remark. Using ultraspherical polynomials, Lewy also showed that there exists a spherical harmonic of even degree whose nodal lines divide the unit sphere into exactly three components.

9.3. Some Facts about Harmonic Maps

In differential geometry, dimension equal to 2 and dimension greater than 2 often give rise to distinct phenomena. For instance, Sacks and Uhlenbeck [56] proved that an isolated singularity of a harmonic map h is removable in two dimensions, if h has finite total energy. This is clearly not true in three dimensions. In this case, an additional condition, such as total energy being small (see [46]), should be introduced.

In this section, we put together a collection of facts about harmonic maps that are relevant to grid generation.

First, we derive the harmonic map equation in the general case when Ω and $\bar{\Omega}$ are equipped with Riemannian metrics g and $\bar{g}$, respectively. Recall that the energy functional of a smooth map u from Ω into $\bar{\Omega}$ is

$$E(u) = \int_M |\nabla u|^2 \, dV.$$

In local coordinates $x \in \Omega$ and $u \in \bar{\Omega}$, the energy density

$$|\nabla u|^2 = g^{\alpha\beta}(x)\frac{\partial u^i}{\partial x^\alpha}\frac{\partial u^j}{\partial x^\beta}\bar{g}_{ij}(u(x)),$$
$$\alpha, \beta = 1, 2, \cdots, \dim \Omega;$$
$$i, j = 1, 2, \cdots, \dim \bar{\Omega}.$$

To simplify the derivation, let $\bar{\Omega}$ be isometrically embedded in $\mathbb{R}^q$ for some q. Let P be the nearest point projection from $\mathbb{R}^q$ into $\bar{\Omega}$.

Let φ be a smooth map from Ω into $\mathbb{R}^q$. Define a one-parameter family of maps u_t from Ω into $\bar{\Omega} \subset \mathbb{R}^q$ by

$$u_t(x) = P(u(x) + t\,\varphi(x))$$

for t near 0. We have

$$\nabla u_t(x)\,|_{t=0} = dP_{u(x)}(\nabla u(x)) = \nabla u(x),$$
$$\frac{d}{dt}u_t(x)\,|_{t=0} = dP_{u(x)}(\varphi(x)).$$

At a critical point $u : \Omega \to \bar{\Omega}$,

$$\frac{d}{dt}E(u_t)\,|_{t=0} \quad (\forall \varphi : \Omega \to \mathbb{R}^q).$$

Thus,

$$0 = \int_\Omega \left\langle \left(\frac{d}{dt}\nabla u_t(x)\right)|_{t=0}, \nabla u(x)\right\rangle dV(x)$$

$$= \int_\Omega \left\langle \nabla\left(\frac{d}{dt}u_t(x)\,|_{t=0}\right), \nabla u(x)\right\rangle dV(x)$$

$$= \int_\Omega \left\langle \nabla\left(dP_{u(x)}(\varphi(x))\right), \nabla u(x)\right\rangle dV(x),$$

$$= \int_\Omega \left\langle d^2 P_{u(x)}(\nabla u(x), \varphi(x)) + dP_{u(x)}(\nabla\varphi(x)), \nabla u(x)\right\rangle dV(x)$$

$$= \int_\Omega \left[\left\langle d^2 P(\nabla u(x), \varphi(x)), \nabla u(x)\right\rangle + \left\langle dP(\nabla u), \nabla\varphi\right\rangle\right] dV(x)$$

$$= \int_\Omega \left\langle d^2 P(\nabla u, \nabla u) - \triangle u, \varphi\right\rangle dV(x),$$

where we have used the facts that d^2P is a symmetric bilinear form and that $\langle dP(\nabla\varphi), \nabla u\rangle = \langle dP(\nabla u), \nabla\varphi\rangle$. Since φ is arbitrary, we get

$$\nabla u - d^2P(\nabla u, \nabla u) = 0.$$

Conclusion. The harmonic map equation (i.e., the Euler–Lagrange equation of the energy functional) is a semilinear elliptic system, quadratic in ∇u. Its leading term is the Laplacian with respect to the Riemannian metric g in Ω. In local coordinates, for a smooth function f on Ω, $\triangle f$ is defined by

$$\triangle f = \frac{1}{\sqrt{\det(g_{\alpha\beta})}} \frac{\partial}{\partial x_\mu} \left(\sqrt{\det(g_{\alpha\beta})}\, g^{\mu\nu}\, \frac{\partial f}{\partial x_\nu}\right).$$

By studying the heat equation

$$\triangle u - \frac{\partial u}{\partial t} - d^2P(\nabla u, \nabla u) = 0,$$

Eells and Sampson [28] proved the fundamental result given in the following theorem.

THEOREM 9.3.1. *Let Ω and $\bar\Omega$ be two Riemannian manifolds without boundary. Let φ be a smooth map from Ω into $\bar\Omega$. Then φ can be continuously deformed into a harmonic map from Ω into $\bar\Omega$ if $\bar\Omega$ has nonpositive sectional curvature.*

This existence theorem was generalized to manifolds with boundary by Hamilton [36].

THEOREM 9.3.2. *Let Ω and $\bar\Omega$ be Riemannian manifolds with boundary. Let φ be a map from Ω into $\bar\Omega$. Then φ can be continuously deformed into a harmonic map from Ω into $\bar\Omega$ if $\bar\Omega$ has nonpositive sectional curvature and if $\partial\bar\Omega$ is convex.*

In this theorem, $\dim\Omega \geq 2$, $\dim\bar\Omega \geq 2$. A few years ago, Lawson and Yau *conjectured* that if u is a harmonic map between two compact Riemannian manifolds of negative curvature, and if u is a homotopy equivalence, then u is a diffeomorphism. This statement has been proven in the case when $\dim\Omega = \dim\bar\Omega = 2$. More precisely, we have Theorems 9.3.3 and 9.3.4, which are due to Schoen and Yau [57].

THEOREM 9.3.3. *Let Ω and $\bar\Omega$ be two Riemann surfaces with the same genus $q \geq 1$. Let Ω have nonpositive curvature. Then, every degree-one harmonic map from Ω into $\bar\Omega$ is a diffeomorphism.*

THEOREM 9.3.4. *In the case when Ω and $\bar\Omega$ have boundary, the same conclusion is true if $\partial\bar\Omega$ has nonnegative geodesic curvature, and if the harmonic map restricted to $\partial\Omega$ is a homeomorphism from $\partial\Omega$ to $\partial\bar\Omega$.*

Remark. The last theorem is a generalization of Rado's theorem to Riemann surfaces. Both Ω and $\bar\Omega$ are two-dimensional.

It should be pointed out that some authors mistakenly quoted the conjecture as a theorem (cf. [25]). In three dimensions, the conjecture is still open. The generalization of Rado's theorem to three dimensions is also not known, which is posed in the following problem:

Let Ω and $\bar{\Omega}$ be simply connected domains in $\mathbb{R}^3$. Let $\bar{\Omega}$ be convex. Let $u : \Omega \to \bar{\Omega}$ be a harmonic map such that $u : \partial\Omega \to \partial\bar{\Omega}$ is a homeomorphism. Is it true that the Jacobian of u does not vanish in the interior of Ω (and consequently u must be a diffeomorphism from Ω to $\bar{\Omega}$)?

Chapter 10

Mathematical Aspects of Harmonic Grid Generation

S. S. Sritharan

10.1. Introduction

Harmonic mapping was one of the earliest and is perhaps the most widely used grid-generation technique in computational physics. Although there is an extensive literature on the theory of harmonic maps on Riemannian manifolds [27], these works do not address the specific questions involved in the harmonic grid-generation method. In [63] a mathematical study of this method was presented. In this chapter we will further elaborate on the underlying mathematical structure of this method and sharpen some of the results. The mathematical analysis presented in [63] is very general and is applicable to nonsmooth domains in Riemannian manifolds as well. In this chapter, however, we will restrict ourselves to smooth domains in Euclidean two and three spaces. New features explored in this chapter are the variational formulation and the concept of duality.

10.2. Variational Formulation

DEFINITION. Let $\Omega \subset \boldsymbol{R}^n$ be a bounded open set with class C^2 boundary $\partial\Omega$, and let $\Omega_1 \subset \boldsymbol{R}^n$ be a bounded *convex* open set with boundary $\partial\Omega_1$. Suppose there exists a continuous transformation $\boldsymbol{\alpha} : \Omega \to \boldsymbol{R}^n$ such that

$$\boldsymbol{\alpha} : \partial\Omega \to \partial\Omega_1$$

is a specified homeomorphism. Then $\boldsymbol{\alpha}$ is called a *grid-generating transform* if

$$\boldsymbol{\alpha} : \bar{\Omega} \to \bar{\Omega}_1$$

is a homeomorphism onto. Ω and Ω_1 are often called the *physical* and the *computational* domains, respectively. Grid-generating transforms belong to a general class of continuous maps known as *regular maps* [23], which map the boundary of the domain onto the boundary of the image.

A grid-generating transform $\boldsymbol{\alpha}$ is *harmonic* if

$$\Delta\boldsymbol{\alpha} = 0.$$

131

Here Δ denotes the Laplacian operator and $\boldsymbol{\alpha} = (\alpha_1, \cdots, \alpha_n)$. Our goal is to find a harmonic grid-generating map for a given domain Ω. We will focus our attention on the cases $n = 2$ and 3, both of which are of practical interest. Let us begin with the following well-known orthogonal decomposition [10] of $L^2(\Omega)$.

$$L^2(\Omega) = \mathcal{H}(\Omega) \oplus \mathcal{G}(\Omega),$$

where

$$\mathcal{H}(\Omega) = \{\boldsymbol{u} \in L^2(\Omega); \nabla \cdot \boldsymbol{u} = 0\},$$

and

$$\mathcal{G}(\Omega) = \{\boldsymbol{u} \in L^2(\Omega); \boldsymbol{u} = \nabla\boldsymbol{\alpha}, \boldsymbol{\alpha} \in H_0^1(\Omega)\}.$$

Here $H_0^1(\Omega)$ denotes the Sobolev space of square-integrable vectorfields (or tensorfields) with square-integrable distributional derivatives and zero boundary values.

Let us define the normal trace operator γ_ν as

$$\gamma_\nu \boldsymbol{u} = \boldsymbol{u} \cdot \boldsymbol{n}|_{\partial\Omega}, \quad \forall \boldsymbol{u} \in C(\bar{\Omega}).$$

The following result is a slightly specialized version of a theorem in [70].

LEMMA 10.2.1. *The trace operator* $\gamma_\nu : \mathcal{H}(\Omega) \to H^{-1/2}(\partial\Omega)$ *continuously. Here* $H^{-1/2}(\partial\Omega)$ *is the dual of the Sobolev space* $H^{1/2}(\partial\Omega)$. *The proof is simple and we will outline it below.*

Proof. Recall that the trace operator γ_0 defined by

$$\gamma_0 \boldsymbol{u} = \boldsymbol{u}|_{\partial\Omega}, \quad \forall \boldsymbol{u} \in C(\bar{\Omega})$$

can be extended as $\gamma_0 : H^1(\Omega) \to H^{1/2}(\partial\Omega)$ continuously. Moreover, the right inverse of this operator $l_\Omega \in \mathcal{L}(H^{1/2}(\partial\Omega); H^1(\Omega))$. Now let the vectorfield $\boldsymbol{u} \in L^2(\Omega)$ be given. Let us consider

$$\chi_u(\phi) = \int_\Omega \boldsymbol{u} \cdot \nabla(l_\Omega\phi)dx, \quad \forall \phi \in H^{1/2}(\partial\Omega).$$

We have, by the Schwartz inequality,

$$\left| \int_\Omega \boldsymbol{u} \cdot \nabla(l_\Omega\phi)dx \right| \leq \|\boldsymbol{u}\|_{L^2(\Omega)} \|l_\Omega\phi\|_{H^1(\Omega)}.$$

Hence

$$|\chi_u(\phi)| \leq C_\Omega \|\boldsymbol{u}\|_{L^2(\Omega)} \|\phi\|_{H^{1/2}(\partial\Omega)}, \quad \forall \phi \in H^{1/2}(\partial\Omega).$$

That is, for each $\boldsymbol{u} \in L^2(\Omega)$ the linear map $\chi_u(\cdot) : H^{1/2}(\partial\Omega) \to \boldsymbol{R}$ continuously. Hence, by the Riesz representation theorem, there exists $\gamma_\nu \boldsymbol{u} \in H^{-1/2}(\partial\Omega)$ such that

$$\int_\Omega \boldsymbol{u} \cdot \nabla(l_\Omega\phi)dx = \langle \gamma_\nu \boldsymbol{u}, \gamma_0\phi \rangle_{H^{-1/2}(\partial\Omega) \times H^{1/2}(\partial\Omega)}.$$

To interpret the element $\gamma_\nu \boldsymbol{u}$, we take $\boldsymbol{u} \in C^1(\bar{\Omega})$ such that $\nabla \cdot \boldsymbol{u} = 0$ and $\phi \in C^1(\bar{\Omega})$. Then, integrating the above integral by parts, we get

$$\langle \gamma_\nu \boldsymbol{u}, \gamma_0 \phi \rangle_{H^{-1/2}(\partial\Omega) \times H^{1/2}(\partial\Omega)} = \int_{\partial\Omega} \boldsymbol{u} \cdot \boldsymbol{n} \phi \, ds.$$

Thus $\gamma_\nu \boldsymbol{u} = \boldsymbol{u} \cdot \boldsymbol{n}|_{\partial\Omega}$, for all $\boldsymbol{u} \in C^1(\bar{\Omega})$. $\qquad \square$

The following result is a special case of a theorem in [64].

LEMMA 10.2.2. *Let Ω be simply connected with boundary $\partial\Omega$ of class $C^r, r \geq m+2, m \geq 0$. Then*

$$\mathrm{curl}\ H^{m+1}(\Omega) = H^m(\Omega) \cap \mathcal{H}(\Omega),$$

and curl is an isomorphism from $H^{m+1}(\Omega)$ onto $H^m(\Omega) \cap \mathcal{H}(\Omega)$.

Let us denote the gradient operator by

$$\Lambda = \mathrm{grad} \quad \text{in } \mathcal{D}(\Omega)',$$

where $\mathcal{D}(\Omega)'$ is the space of distributions (dual to the space of test functions $\mathcal{D}(\Omega)$).

LEMMA 10.2.3. $\Lambda \in \mathcal{L}(H^1(\Omega); L^2(\Omega))$ *and its transpose* $\Lambda^* \in \mathcal{L}(L^2(\Omega); (H^1(\Omega))')$. *Moreover, if we restrict Λ to $H_0^1(\Omega)$, then denoting its transpose by $\Lambda_1^* \in \mathcal{L}(L^2(\Omega); H^{-1}(\Omega))$, we get $\Lambda_1^* = $div in $\mathcal{D}(\Omega)'$.*

Proof. Let us note that by the Schwartz inequality we have

$$\left| \int_\Omega \nabla \boldsymbol{\alpha} \cdot \boldsymbol{Q} \, dx \right| \leq \|\boldsymbol{\alpha}\|_{H^1(\Omega)} \|\boldsymbol{Q}\|_{L^2(\Omega)}, \quad \forall \boldsymbol{\alpha} \in H^1(\Omega) \quad \text{and} \quad \forall \boldsymbol{Q} \in L^2(\Omega).$$

Hence, for a given tensorfield $\boldsymbol{Q} \in L^2(\Omega)$,

$$\left| \int_\Omega \nabla \boldsymbol{\alpha} \cdot \boldsymbol{Q} \, dx \right| \leq C \|\boldsymbol{\alpha}\|_{H^1(\Omega)}, \quad \forall \boldsymbol{\alpha} \in H^1(\Omega).$$

Thus, by the Riesz representation theorem, there exists a vectorfield $\boldsymbol{\beta}^* \in (H^1(\Omega))'$ such that

$$\int_\Omega \nabla \boldsymbol{\alpha} \cdot \boldsymbol{Q} \, dx = \langle \boldsymbol{\beta}^*, \boldsymbol{\alpha} \rangle_{(H^1(\Omega))' \times H^1(\Omega)}.$$

This defines a unique operator $\Lambda^* \in \mathcal{L}(L^2(\Omega); (H^1(\Omega))')$ such that $\boldsymbol{\beta}^* = \Lambda^* \boldsymbol{Q}$ and

$$(\boldsymbol{Q}, \Lambda \boldsymbol{\alpha})_{L^2(\Omega)} = \langle \Lambda^* \boldsymbol{Q}, \boldsymbol{\alpha} \rangle_{(H^1(\Omega))' \times H^1(\Omega)},$$
$$\forall \boldsymbol{\alpha} \in H^1(\Omega) \quad \text{and} \quad \forall \boldsymbol{Q} \in L^2(\Omega).$$

Since the above estimate on the integral holds also for all $\boldsymbol{\alpha} \in H_0^1(\Omega)$, we can define $\Lambda_1^* \in \mathcal{L}(L^2(\Omega); H^{-1}(\Omega))$ such that

$$(\boldsymbol{Q}, \Lambda \boldsymbol{\alpha})_{L^2(\Omega)} = \langle \Lambda_1^* \boldsymbol{Q}, \boldsymbol{\alpha} \rangle_{H^{-1}(\Omega) \times H^1(\Omega)},$$
$$\forall \boldsymbol{\alpha} \in H_0^1(\Omega) \quad \text{and} \quad \forall \boldsymbol{Q} \in L^2(\Omega).$$

Now, note that integration by parts gives

$$\int_\Omega \nabla\alpha \cdot Q dx = -\int_\Omega \alpha \cdot \operatorname{div} Q dx, \qquad \forall \alpha \in \mathcal{D}(\Omega) \quad \text{and} \quad \forall Q \in \mathcal{D}(\Omega).$$

Hence $\Lambda_1^* = -\operatorname{div}$ in $\mathcal{D}(\Omega)'$. Note, however, that

$$\int_\Omega \nabla\alpha \cdot Q dx = -\int_\Omega \alpha \cdot \operatorname{div} Q dx + \int_{\partial\Omega} \alpha \cdot Q \cdot n dS,$$
$$\forall \alpha \in C^1(\bar\Omega) \quad \text{and} \quad \forall Q \in C^1(\bar\Omega).$$

This explains the difference between Λ_1^* and Λ^*.   □

We will now provide a variational formulation for our grid-generation problem. Let us denote by $\mathcal{A} \subset H^1(\Omega)$ the closed convex subset defined as

$$\mathcal{A} = \alpha_0 + H_0^1(\Omega),$$

where $\alpha_0 \in H^1(\Omega)$ is such that

$$\alpha_0|_{\partial\Omega} = g \in H^{1/2}(\partial\Omega)$$

with a given boundary distribution of a vectorfield g.

Let us denote by $\delta(\alpha|\mathcal{A})$ the indicator function defined as

$$\delta(\alpha|\mathcal{A}) = \begin{cases} 0, & \text{if } \alpha \in \mathcal{A} \\ +\infty, & \text{otherwise.} \end{cases}$$

PROBLEM 10.2.1 (primal variational problem). *Find a vectorfield* $\alpha : \Omega \to R^n$ *such that* $\alpha \in H^1(\Omega)$ *and*

$$(10.1) \qquad \mathcal{J}(\alpha) = \tfrac{1}{2}\|\Lambda\alpha\|_{L^2(\Omega)}^2 + \delta(\alpha|\mathcal{A}) \to \inf.$$

Here $\nabla\alpha$ is written componentwise as

$$\frac{\partial\alpha_i}{\partial x^j}, \qquad i,j = 1,\cdots,n.$$

and

$$\|\Lambda\alpha\|_{L^2(\Omega)}^2 = \int_\Omega |\nabla\alpha|^2 dx = \sum_{ij=1}^n \int_\Omega \left|\frac{\partial\alpha_i}{\partial x^j}\right|^2 dx.$$

Note that in this variational formulation we are looking for a solution such that $\alpha - \alpha_0 \in \mathcal{G}(\Omega)$.

Let us now consider the dual formulation.

PROBLEM 10.2.2 (dual variational problem). *Find a tensorfield* $Q^* : \Omega \to R^n \times R^n$ *such that* $Q^* \in \mathcal{H}(\Omega)$ *and*

$$(10.2) \quad \mathcal{J}^*(Q^*) = \langle\gamma_\nu Q^*, g\rangle_{H^{-1/2}(\partial\Omega)\times H^{1/2}(\partial\Omega)} - \tfrac{1}{2}\|Q^*\|_{L^2(\Omega)}^2 \to \sup.$$

Here $\boldsymbol{Q}^* \in \mathcal{H}(\Omega)$ implies that

$$\sum_{ij=1}^{n} \int_{\Omega} (Q_{ij}^*)^2 dx < \infty \quad \text{and} \quad [\nabla \cdot \boldsymbol{Q}^*]_i = \frac{\partial Q_{ij}^*}{\partial x^j} = 0, \qquad i = 1, \cdots, n.$$

Moreover, the duality pairing

$$\langle \gamma_\nu \boldsymbol{Q}^*, \boldsymbol{g} \rangle_{H^{-1/2}(\partial\Omega) \times H^{1/2}(\partial\Omega)} = \sum_{ij=1}^{n} \int_{\partial\Omega} Q_{ij}^* n_j g_i dS.$$

Let us now verify that this dual variational principle can be derived from the primal problem using the concept of polar functions [5]. We will begin with the following *perturbed variational problem* obtained from the primal problem.

Let $\boldsymbol{Q} \in L^2(\Omega)$ be a tensorfield. Let us find $\boldsymbol{\alpha} \in H^1(\Omega)$ such that

$$(10.3) \qquad \Phi(\boldsymbol{\alpha}, \boldsymbol{Q}) = \tfrac{1}{2}\|\Lambda\boldsymbol{\alpha} + \boldsymbol{Q}\|_{L^2(\Omega)}^2 + \delta(\boldsymbol{\alpha}|\mathcal{A}) \to \inf.$$

We define the *value function* $\mathcal{V}(\cdot) : L^2(\Omega) \to \boldsymbol{R}$ as

$$(10.4) \qquad \mathcal{V}(\boldsymbol{Q}) = \inf_{\alpha \in H^1(\Omega)} \Phi(\boldsymbol{\alpha}, \boldsymbol{Q}).$$

Note that $\mathcal{V}(0)$ corresponds to the primal problem. We now note that the polar function corresponding to $\Phi(\cdot, \cdot)$ is

$$\Phi^*(\boldsymbol{\alpha}^*, \boldsymbol{Q}^*) = \sup_{\alpha \in H^1(\Omega)} \sup_{Q \in L^2(\Omega)} \{\langle \boldsymbol{\alpha}^*, \boldsymbol{\alpha} \rangle_{(H^1(\Omega))' \times H^1(\Omega)} + (\boldsymbol{Q}^*, \boldsymbol{Q})_{L^2(\Omega)} - \Phi(\boldsymbol{\alpha}, \boldsymbol{Q})\}.$$

We will show below that the dual problem is actually that of finding $\boldsymbol{Q}^* \in L^2(\Omega)$ such that

$$(10.5) \qquad -\Phi^*(0, \boldsymbol{Q}^*) \to \sup.$$

Let us first establish the following relationship between $\Phi^*(0, \boldsymbol{Q}^*)$ and the bidual of the value function $\mathcal{V}^{**}(\cdot)$:

$$(10.6) \qquad \mathcal{V}^{**}(0) = \sup_{Q^* \in L^2(\Omega)} \{-\Phi^*(0, \boldsymbol{Q}^*)\}.$$

In fact, if we consider

$$\mathcal{V}^*(\boldsymbol{Q}^*) = \sup_{Q \in L^2(\Omega)} \{(\boldsymbol{Q}^*, \boldsymbol{Q})_{L^2(\Omega)} - \mathcal{V}(\boldsymbol{Q})\}$$

and

$$\mathcal{V}^{**}(\boldsymbol{Q}^{**}) = \sup_{Q^* \in L^2(\Omega)} \{(\boldsymbol{Q}^{**}, \boldsymbol{Q}^*)_{L^2(\Omega)} - \mathcal{V}^*(\boldsymbol{Q}^*)\},$$

then

$$\mathcal{V}^{**}(0) = \sup_{Q^* \in L^2(\Omega)} \{-\mathcal{V}^*(\boldsymbol{Q}^*)\}$$

$$= \sup_{Q^* \in L^2(\Omega)} \{- \sup_{Q \in L^2(\Omega)} \{(\boldsymbol{Q}^*, \boldsymbol{Q})_{L^2(\Omega)} - \mathcal{V}(\boldsymbol{Q})\}\}$$

$$= \sup_{Q^* \in L^2(\Omega)} \{- \sup_{Q \in L^2(\Omega)} \{(\boldsymbol{Q}^*, \boldsymbol{Q})_{L^2(\Omega)} - \inf_{\alpha \in H^1(\Omega)} \Phi(\boldsymbol{\alpha}, \boldsymbol{Q})\}\}$$

$$= \sup_{Q^* \in L^2(\Omega)} \{- \sup_{Q \in L^2(\Omega)} \sup_{\alpha \in H^1(\Omega)} \{(\boldsymbol{Q}^*, \boldsymbol{Q})_{L^2(\Omega)} - \Phi(\boldsymbol{\alpha}, \boldsymbol{Q})\}\}.$$

Hence

$$\mathcal{V}^{**}(0) = \sup_{Q^* \in L^2(\Omega)} \{-\Phi^*(0, Q^*)\},$$

which verifies (10.6). We will now consider

$$\Phi^*(0, Q^*) = \sup_{Q \in L^2(\Omega)} \sup_{\alpha \in H^1(\Omega)} \{(Q^*, Q)_{L^2(\Omega)} - \tfrac{1}{2}\|\Lambda\alpha + Q\|^2_{L^2(\Omega)} - \delta(\alpha|\mathcal{A})\}$$

$$= \sup_{Q \in L^2(\Omega)} \sup_{\alpha \in H^1(\Omega)} \{(Q^*, Q + \Lambda\alpha)_{L^2(\Omega)} - \tfrac{1}{2}\|Q + \Lambda\alpha\|^2_{L^2(\Omega)}$$

$$- (\Lambda\alpha, Q^*)_{L^2(\Omega)} - \delta(\alpha|\mathcal{A})\}$$

$$= \sup_{P \in L^2(\Omega)} \{(Q^*, P)_{L^2(\Omega)} - \tfrac{1}{2}\|P\|^2_{L^2(\Omega)}\}$$

$$+ \sup_{\alpha \in H^1(\Omega)} \{\langle -\Lambda^* Q^*, \alpha\rangle_{(H^1(\Omega))' \times H^1(\Omega)} - \delta(\alpha|\mathcal{A})\} = \tfrac{1}{2}\|Q^*\|^2_{L^2(\Omega)}$$

$$+ \delta^*(-\Lambda^* Q^*|\mathcal{A}),$$

where $\delta^*(\cdot|\mathcal{A})$ is the polar of the indicator function $\delta(\cdot|\mathcal{A})$. Hence (10.6) becomes

$$\mathcal{V}^{**}(0) = \sup_{Q^* \in L^2(\Omega)} \{-\tfrac{1}{2}\|Q^*\|^2_{L^2(\Omega)} - \delta^*(-\Lambda^* Q^*|\mathcal{A})\}.$$

Let us consider

$$\delta^*(-\Lambda^* Q^*|\mathcal{A}) = \sup_{\alpha \in \mathcal{A}} \langle -\Lambda^* Q^*, \alpha\rangle_{(H^1(\Omega))' \times H^1(\Omega)}.$$

Since $\alpha = \alpha_0 + \beta$, where $\alpha_0 \in H^1(\Omega)$ was defined earlier, and $\beta \in H^1_0(\Omega)$, we get

$$\delta^*(-\Lambda^* Q^*|\mathcal{A}) = \langle -\Lambda^* Q^*, \alpha_0\rangle_{(H^1(\Omega))' \times H^1(\Omega)}$$

$$+ \sup_{\beta \in H^1_0(\Omega)} \langle -\Lambda^*_1 Q^*, \beta\rangle_{H^{-1}(\Omega) \times H^1_0(\Omega)}.$$

Note that

$$\sup_{\beta \in H^1_0(\Omega)} \langle -\Lambda^*_1 Q^*, \beta\rangle_{H^{-1}(\Omega) \times H^1_0(\Omega)} = \begin{cases} 0, & \text{if } \Lambda^*_1 Q^* = 0 \\ +\infty, & \text{otherwise.} \end{cases}$$

Hence

$$\sup_{Q^* \in L^2(\Omega)} \{-\delta^*(-\Lambda^* Q^*|\mathcal{A})\} = \sup_{Q^* \in L^2(\Omega)} \{-\langle -\Lambda^* Q^*, \alpha_0\rangle_{(H^1(\Omega))' \times H^1(\Omega)} - 0\},$$

with $\Lambda^*_1 Q^* = 0$. Thus

$$\mathcal{V}^{**}(0) = \sup_{Q^* \in L^2(\Omega)} \{-\tfrac{1}{2}\|Q^*\|^2 + \langle \Lambda^* Q^*, \alpha_0\rangle_{(H^1(\Omega))' \times H^1(\Omega)}\},$$

with $\Lambda_1^* Q^* = 0$. Let us further interpret this result:

$$\Lambda_1^* Q^* = \operatorname{div} Q^* = 0.$$

Hence, $Q^* \in \mathcal{H}(\Omega)$ and this implies, by Lemma 10.2.1, that $\gamma_\nu Q^* \in H^{-1/2}(\partial\Omega)$. Thus we can write

$$\langle \Lambda^* Q^*, \alpha_0 \rangle_{(H^1(\Omega))' \times H^1(\Omega)} = (Q^*, \Lambda\alpha_0)_{L^2(\Omega)} = \int_\Omega Q^* \cdot \nabla\alpha_0 dx$$

$$= -\int_\Omega \alpha_0 \cdot \operatorname{div} Q^* dx + \int_{\partial\Omega} g \cdot Q^* \cdot n dS,$$

from which we get

$$\langle \Lambda^* Q^*, \alpha_0 \rangle_{(H^1(\Omega))' \times H^1(\Omega)} = \int_{\partial\Omega} g \cdot Q^* \cdot n dS = \langle \gamma_\nu Q^*, g \rangle_{H^{-1/2}(\partial\Omega) \times H^{1/2}(\partial\Omega)}.$$

Thus

$$(10.7) \quad \mathcal{V}^{**}(0) = \sup_{Q^* \in \mathcal{H}(\Omega)} \{ -\tfrac{1}{2} \|Q^*\|^2 + \langle \gamma_\nu Q^*, g \rangle_{H^{-1/2}(\partial\Omega) \times H^{1/2}(\partial\Omega)} \}.$$

This is precisely the dual problem.

Let us now state the following relevant theorem.

THEOREM 10.2.1. *There exist unique solutions $\hat{\alpha}$ and $\hat{Q}^*$, which correspond, respectively, to the primal and the dual problems such that*

$$\inf_{\alpha \in H^1(\Omega)} \mathcal{J}(\alpha) = \mathcal{J}(\hat{\alpha}) = \sup_{Q^* \in \mathcal{H}(\Omega)} \mathcal{J}^*(Q^*) = \mathcal{J}^*(\hat{Q}^*),$$

with $\hat{Q}^* = \nabla\hat{\alpha}$. The vectorfield $\hat{\alpha}$ satisfies $\Delta\hat{\alpha} = 0$ in the sense of distributions and

$$\gamma_0 \hat{\alpha} = \hat{\alpha}|_{\partial\Omega} = g \quad \text{in the sense of trace.}$$

Moreover, there exists a tensorfield $\hat{\psi} \in H^1(\Omega)$ such that

$$\nabla\hat{\alpha} = \operatorname{curl} \hat{\psi} \in \mathcal{H}(\Omega).$$

Proof. Let us first note that the perturbed variational problem (10.3) has a unique solution α_Q for each $Q \in L^2(\Omega)$, including for $Q = 0$, which corresponds to the primal problem. This is essentially the Dirichlet principle, and we simply note the main arguments leading to this result. Since the set $\mathcal{A}$ is closed, the epigraph

$$epi\delta(\cdot|\mathcal{A}) = \{(\alpha, a) \in H^1(\Omega) \times \boldsymbol{R} | \delta(\alpha|\mathcal{A}) \le a\}$$

is closed and hence the indicator function $\delta(\cdot|\mathcal{A}) : H^1(\Omega) \to \boldsymbol{R} \cup \{+\infty\}$ is lower semicontinuous. Moreover, this is a convex function since $\mathcal{A}$ is convex. The convexity and lower semicontinuity of $\delta(\cdot|\mathcal{A})$ imply that this function is also weakly sequentially lower semicontinuous in $H^1(\Omega)$. We therefore conclude that for all $\boldsymbol{Q} \in L^2(\Omega)$, the function $\Phi(\cdot, \boldsymbol{Q}) : H^1(\Omega) \to \boldsymbol{R} \cup \{+\infty\}$ is convex and weakly sequentially lower semicontinuous. Hence we can deduce by standard compactness arguments that for each $\boldsymbol{Q} \in L^2(\Omega)$, there exists a unique solution $\hat{\boldsymbol{\alpha}}_Q$ such that

$$\mathcal{V}(\boldsymbol{Q}) = \inf_{\alpha \in H^1(\Omega)} \Phi(\alpha, \boldsymbol{Q}) = \Phi(\hat{\boldsymbol{\alpha}}_Q, \boldsymbol{Q}).$$

This shows that for each $\boldsymbol{Q} \in L^2(\Omega)$ the value function is defined with a unique element $\hat{\boldsymbol{\alpha}}_Q \in \mathcal{A}$. Setting $\boldsymbol{Q} = 0$ gives us the existence of a unique solution $\hat{\boldsymbol{\alpha}}$ to the primal problem.

From (10.4), (10.6), and (10.7) we know that in order to establish the coincidence of the primal and dual problems, we need to show that

$$\mathcal{V}(0) = \mathcal{V}^{**}(0).$$

We will now examine the properties of the value function to deduce this result. Note that $\Phi(\cdot, \cdot) : H^1(\Omega) \times L^2(\Omega) \to \boldsymbol{R} \cup \{+\infty\}$ is convex and this implies that the value function $\mathcal{V}(\cdot) : L^2(\Omega) \to \boldsymbol{R}$ is convex.

Now, let us consider a sequence $\boldsymbol{Q}^n \to 0$ weakly in $L^2(\Omega)$. Then, since for all n, $\hat{\boldsymbol{\alpha}}_Q^n \in \mathcal{A}$, we have

$$\mathcal{V}(\boldsymbol{Q}^n) = \Phi(\hat{\boldsymbol{\alpha}}_Q^n, \boldsymbol{Q}^n) = \tfrac{1}{2}\|\Lambda\hat{\boldsymbol{\alpha}}_Q^n + \boldsymbol{Q}^n\|_{L^2(\Omega)}^2.$$

Now, using the estimate

$$\|\Lambda\hat{\boldsymbol{\alpha}}_Q^n\|_{L^2(\Omega)} \leq C(\|\boldsymbol{Q}^n\|_{L^2(\Omega)}, \|g\|_{H^{1/2}(\partial\Omega)})$$

and the fact that Λ is a closed operator in $H^1(\Omega)$, we can conclude that $\Lambda\hat{\boldsymbol{\alpha}}_Q^n \to \Lambda\alpha$ weakly in $L^2(\Omega)$. Thus $\Lambda\hat{\boldsymbol{\alpha}}_Q^n + \boldsymbol{Q}^n \to \Lambda\alpha$ weakly in $L^2(\Omega)$. We then conclude that

$$\mathcal{V}(0) \leq \liminf_{n\to\infty} \mathcal{V}(\boldsymbol{Q}^n),$$

which establishes the lower semicontinuity of $\mathcal{V}(\cdot)$ at the origin. This, in combination with the fact that $\mathcal{V}(\cdot)$ is a convex function, implies [5] that

$$\mathcal{V}(0) = \mathcal{V}^{**}(0)$$

and hence the primal and dual problems have the same values:

$$\inf_{\alpha \in H^1(\Omega)} \mathcal{J}(\alpha) = \mathcal{J}(\hat{\alpha}) = \sup_{Q^* \in \mathcal{H}(\Omega)} \mathcal{J}^*(\boldsymbol{Q}^*) = \mathcal{J}^*(\hat{\boldsymbol{Q}}^*).$$

Let us now derive an implication of this *optimality relationship*. We have, for the optimal solutions $\hat{\alpha} \in \mathcal{A}$ and $\hat{\boldsymbol{Q}}^* \in \mathcal{H}(\Omega)$,

$$\tfrac{1}{2}\|\Lambda\hat{\alpha}\|_{L^2(\Omega)}^2 = -\tfrac{1}{2}\|\hat{\boldsymbol{Q}}^*\|_{L^2(\Omega)}^2 + \langle\gamma_\nu\hat{\boldsymbol{Q}}^*, g\rangle_{H^{-1/2}(\partial\Omega)\times H^{1/2}(\partial\Omega)}.$$

That is,

$$(10.8) \qquad \tfrac{1}{2}\|\Lambda\hat{\alpha} - \hat{\boldsymbol{Q}}^*\|_{L^2(\Omega)}^2 + (\Lambda\hat{\alpha}, \hat{\boldsymbol{Q}}^*)_{L^2(\Omega)}$$
$$- \langle\gamma_\nu\hat{\boldsymbol{Q}}^*, g\rangle_{H^{-1/2}(\partial\Omega)\times H^{1/2}(\partial\Omega)} = 0.$$

But

$$(\Lambda\hat{\boldsymbol{\alpha}}, \hat{\boldsymbol{Q}}^*)_{L^2(\Omega)} = -\langle \ \Lambda_1^*\boldsymbol{Q}^*, \hat{\boldsymbol{\alpha}}\rangle_{H^{-1}(\Omega)\times H^1(\Omega)}$$
$$+ \langle \gamma_\nu\hat{\boldsymbol{Q}}^*, \boldsymbol{g}\rangle_{H^{-1/2}(\partial\Omega)\times H^{1/2}(\partial\Omega)}$$

with $\Lambda_1^*\boldsymbol{Q}^* = \mathrm{div}\boldsymbol{Q}^* = 0$. Thus (10.8) becomes

$$\|\Lambda\hat{\boldsymbol{\alpha}} - \hat{\boldsymbol{Q}}^*\|_{L^2(\Omega)} = 0,$$

and we conclude that
(10.9) $$\Lambda\hat{\boldsymbol{\alpha}} = \hat{\boldsymbol{Q}}^* \in \mathcal{H}(\Omega).$$

Now, since $\mathcal{H}(\Omega) = curl\ H^1(\Omega)$ by Lemma 10.2.2, we can deduce that there exists a tensorfield $\hat{\boldsymbol{\psi}} \in H^1(\Omega)$ such that

(10.10) $$\mathrm{grad}\ \hat{\boldsymbol{\alpha}} = \mathrm{curl}\ \hat{\boldsymbol{\psi}}.$$

This can also be written in the tensor form as

$$\frac{\partial\hat{\alpha}_i}{\partial x^j} = \epsilon_{jlm}\frac{\partial\hat{\psi}_{mi}}{\partial x^l}, \qquad i,j = 1,2,3.$$

Moreover, $\nabla\hat{\boldsymbol{\alpha}} \in \mathcal{H}(\Omega)$ and hence $\mathrm{div}\ \nabla\hat{\boldsymbol{\alpha}} = 0$. That is,

$$\Delta\hat{\boldsymbol{\alpha}} = 0.$$

Remark. If $n = 2$, we have $\hat{\psi}_{mi} = \delta_{m3}\psi_i$, and then (10.10) becomes

$$\frac{\partial\hat{\alpha}_i}{\partial x^j} = \epsilon_{jl3}\frac{\partial\hat{\psi}_i}{\partial x^l}, \qquad i,j = 1,2.$$

This is the same as

(10.11) $$\frac{\partial\hat{\alpha}_i}{\partial x^1} = \frac{\partial\hat{\psi}_i}{\partial x^2} \quad \text{and} \quad \frac{\partial\hat{\alpha}_i}{\partial x^2} = -\frac{\partial\hat{\psi}_i}{\partial x^1}, \qquad i = 1,2.$$

This is the Cauchy–Riemann relationship and hence for $n = 2$, $\hat{\psi}_i$ is the complex conjugate of $\hat{\alpha}_i$. We also have for $n = 2$,

$$\Delta\hat{\boldsymbol{\alpha}} = \Delta\hat{\boldsymbol{\psi}} = 0.$$

Let us now state a regularity theorem for the vectorfields $\hat{\boldsymbol{\alpha}}$ and $\hat{\boldsymbol{\psi}}$.

THEOREM 10.2.2. *Let $\partial\Omega \in C^{m+2}, m \geq 2$, and $\boldsymbol{g} \in H^{m-1/2}(\partial\Omega)$. Then the optimal solutions have the regularity $\hat{\boldsymbol{\alpha}}, \hat{\boldsymbol{\psi}} \in H^m(\Omega)$.*

Proof. First note that $\hat{\boldsymbol{\alpha}}$ solves

$$\Delta\hat{\boldsymbol{\alpha}} = 0 \quad \text{with} \quad \hat{\boldsymbol{\alpha}}|_{\partial\Omega} = \boldsymbol{g} \in H^{m-1/2}(\partial\Omega).$$

Hence, by standard regularity theory of the Dirichlet problem, we have $\hat{\boldsymbol{\alpha}} \in H^m(\Omega)$. Thus, $\Lambda\hat{\boldsymbol{\alpha}} = curl\hat{\boldsymbol{\psi}} \in H^{m-1}(\Omega) \cap \mathcal{H}(\Omega)$. But $curl$ is an isomorphism from $H^m(\Omega)$ onto $H^{m-1}(\Omega) \cap \mathcal{H}(\Omega)$. Thus $\hat{\boldsymbol{\psi}} \in H^m(\Omega)$. $\square$

10.3. Harmonic Grids in Two Dimensions

In this section, we will present a refined version of the theory presented in [63]. The corresponding theory for three-dimensional domains will be discussed in the next section. *The results in this section will establish that the harmonic map in two dimensions is a grid-generating transform.*

Let us first study some properties of the Jacobian and gradient maps to gain some intuition into the harmonic grid-generation problem. We will demonstrate, in particular, the apparent importance of the convexity of the computational domain Ω_1.

Let the Jacobians associated with the primal and dual problems be denoted as follows:

$$J_\alpha(\boldsymbol{x}) = \text{ Det } \nabla \boldsymbol{\alpha} = \frac{\partial(\alpha_1, \alpha_2)}{\partial(x^1, x^2)},$$

$$J_\psi(\boldsymbol{x}) = \text{ Det } \nabla \boldsymbol{\psi} = \frac{\partial(\psi_1, \psi_2)}{\partial(x^1, x^2)}.$$

LEMMA 10.3.1. *If $\boldsymbol{\alpha}$ and $\boldsymbol{\psi}$ are the optimal solutions of the primal and dual problems, respectively, then*

(i) $J_\alpha(\boldsymbol{x}) = J_\psi(\boldsymbol{x})$,
(ii) *the functions* $|\nabla \alpha_i|^2 = |\nabla \psi_i|^2$, $i = 1, 2$, *are subharmonic, and*
(iii) *the following functions are harmonic:*

$$\frac{J_\alpha(\boldsymbol{x})}{|\nabla \alpha_i|^2} = \frac{J_\psi(\boldsymbol{x})}{|\nabla \psi_i|^2}, \qquad i = 1, 2.$$

Proof. Consider

$$J_\alpha(\boldsymbol{x}) = \frac{\partial \alpha_1}{\partial x^1} \frac{\partial \alpha_2}{\partial x^2} - \frac{\partial \alpha_1}{\partial x^2} \frac{\partial \alpha_2}{\partial x^1}.$$

Using the Cauchy–Riemann relationship (10.11), we get

$$J_\alpha(\boldsymbol{x}) = \left(\frac{\partial \psi_1}{\partial x^2}\right)\left(-\frac{\partial \psi_2}{\partial x^1}\right) - \left(-\frac{\partial \psi_1}{\partial x^1}\right)\left(\frac{\partial \psi_2}{\partial x^2}\right) = J_\psi(\boldsymbol{x}).$$

Note that the Cauchy–Riemann relationships also imply that

$$|\nabla \alpha_i|^2 = \left(\frac{\partial \alpha_i}{\partial x^1}\right)^2 + \left(\frac{\partial \alpha_i}{\partial x^2}\right)^2 = \left(\frac{\partial \psi_i}{\partial x^2}\right)^2 + \left(-\frac{\partial \psi_i}{\partial x^1}\right)^2 = |\nabla \psi_i|^2, \qquad i = 1, 2.$$

Moreover, note that $\partial \alpha_i / \partial x^j$ and $\partial \psi_i / \partial x^j$ are harmonic. It is well known that if a function ϕ is harmonic, then ϕ^2 is subharmonic. In fact,

$$\Delta(\phi^2) = 2\phi\Delta\phi + 2(\nabla\phi)^2$$

$$= 2(\nabla\phi)^2 \geq 0.$$

We thus conclude that

$$\Delta(|\nabla \alpha_i|^2) \geq 0$$

and

$$\Delta(|\nabla \psi_i|^2) \geq 0, \quad \text{for } i = 1, 2.$$

Let us now set $z = x^1 + ix^2$ and consider the complex analytic function

$$W(z) = \left(\frac{\partial \alpha_1}{\partial x^1} + i\frac{\partial \psi_1}{\partial x^1}\right)\left(\frac{\partial \alpha_2}{\partial x^2} + i\frac{\partial \psi_2}{\partial x^2}\right)^{-1}.$$

Using the Cauchy–Riemann relationship we get,

$$W(z) = \left(\frac{\partial \alpha_1}{\partial x^1} - i\frac{\partial \alpha_1}{\partial x^2}\right)\left(\frac{\partial \alpha_2}{\partial x^2} + i\frac{\partial \alpha_2}{\partial x^1}\right)^{-1}.$$

Hence, the real part of $W(z)$ is

$$\Re W(z) = \frac{\partial(\alpha_1, \alpha_2)}{\partial(x^1, x^2)}/|\nabla \alpha_2|^2$$

and is harmonic. We can similarly show that the other functions in (iii) are harmonic.   □

Let us define $\Theta \subset \Omega$ to be a subdomain defined as

$$\Theta = \{x \in \Omega; \text{ dist}(x, \partial\Omega) \geq \delta\}$$

for some $\delta > 0$. Let us take the data on $\partial\Omega$ to be $g \in H^{3/2+\epsilon}(\partial\Omega)$. Then, by the regularity results, we have $\alpha \in H^{2+\epsilon}(\Omega) \subset C^1(\bar{\Omega})$. The following estimate holds:

$$0 \leq \sup_{\bar{\Theta}} |\nabla \alpha| \leq C(\|g\|_{H^{3/2+\epsilon}(\partial\Omega)}).$$

See also [54] for a similar estimate using maximum principle. We note here that even if $|\nabla \alpha_i| > 0$ on $\partial\Theta$, it can vanish inside Θ, since $|\nabla \alpha_i|^2$ is only subharmonic. Lemma 10.3.2 below shows the condition under which we obtain nonvanishing gradients.

Let us assume for the moment that the following estimates hold:

(10.12)
$$0 < C_1 < |\nabla \alpha_i|^2 < C_2, \quad \forall x \in \bar{\Theta}$$

and on the bounding curve $\partial\Theta$,

(10.13)
$$0 < d_1 < J_\alpha(x) < d_2, \quad \forall x \in \partial\Theta.$$

Here C_i, d_i depend on the data g. We then have

$$\frac{d_1}{C_2} < \frac{J_\alpha(x)}{|\nabla \alpha_i|^2} < \frac{d_2}{C_1}, \quad \forall x \in \partial\Theta.$$

Now note that since $J_\alpha(x)/|\nabla \alpha_i|^2$ is a harmonic function, the maximum (and minimum) principle gives

(10.14)
$$\frac{d_1}{C_2} < \frac{J_\alpha(x)}{|\nabla \alpha_i|^2} < \frac{d_2}{C_1}, \quad \forall x \in \bar{\Theta}.$$

From (10.12) and (10.14), we get

$$0 < d_1 < J_\alpha(\boldsymbol{x}) < d_2, \quad \forall \boldsymbol{x} \in \bar{\Theta}.$$

A similar conclusion holds for the dual map $\boldsymbol{\psi}$.

Let us now indicate the condition under which a result of the type (10.12) (actually with $C_1 = 0$) holds.

LEMMA 10.3.2. *Let the optimal solution* $\boldsymbol{\alpha}$ *map* Θ *onto a convex domain* Θ_1. *Then* $\nabla\alpha_i$ *do not vanish in* Θ

Proof. Suppose that $\nabla\alpha_1 = 0$ at $z_0 \in \Theta$. Then $U(z) = \alpha_1 + i\psi_1$ must satisfy

$$\frac{\partial U}{\partial z} = 0 \quad \text{at } z_0,$$

which implies that $\hat{U}(z) = U(z) - U(z_0)$ should have a zero of order greater than or equal to two. If this is true, then the argument of $\hat{U}(z)$ around $\partial\Theta$ is at least 4π, which means that $\alpha_1(z) - \alpha_1(z_0)$ should vanish at least four times on $\partial\Theta$. But the image Θ_1 is convex; therefore this function has exactly two zeros on $\partial\Theta$. From this contradiction we conclude that $\nabla\alpha_1$ and $\nabla\alpha_2$ are never zero in Θ.   □

The above arguments indicate in an intuitive way the reasons for choosing Ω_1 to be convex.

Let us now describe the main theory of this section. The central result is the following theorem.

THEOREM 10.3.1. *Let* $\Omega \subset \boldsymbol{R}^2$ *be a bounded open set with class* C^2 *boundary* $\partial\Omega$, *and let* $\Omega_1 \subset \boldsymbol{R}^2$ *be a bounded convex open set. Let the homeomorphism* $\boldsymbol{\alpha} : \partial\Omega \to \partial\Omega_1$ *be specified by*

$$\boldsymbol{\alpha}|_{\partial\Omega} = \boldsymbol{g} \in H^{3/2+\epsilon}(\partial\Omega), \qquad \epsilon > 0.$$

Then, the optimal solution $\boldsymbol{\alpha}$ *of Theorem* 10.2.1 *is a homeomorphism from* $\bar{\Omega}$ *onto* $\bar{\Omega}_1$.

Proof. The proof of this theorem will be accomplished using three lemmas. We will observe that the stated regularity $\boldsymbol{g} \in H^{3/2+\epsilon}(\partial\Omega)$ is not really required for all of these lemmas.

LEMMA 10.3.3. *Let the optimal solution* $\boldsymbol{\alpha}$ *be obtained by specifying the boundary homeomorphism* $\boldsymbol{\alpha} : \partial\Omega \to \partial\Omega_1$:

$$\boldsymbol{\alpha}|_{\partial\Omega} = \boldsymbol{g} \in H^{1/2+\epsilon}(\partial\Omega).$$

Then $\boldsymbol{\alpha}$ *maps* $\bar{\Omega}$ *onto* $\bar{\Omega}_1$.

Proof. Note that from the regularity results we have for $\epsilon > 0$, $\boldsymbol{\alpha} \in H^{1+\epsilon}(\Omega) \subset C(\bar{\Omega})$, and hence the weak-maximum principle holds [39]. This result and the fact that Ω_1 is convex imply that $\boldsymbol{\alpha}(\Omega) \subseteq \Omega_1$. To see this, first note that the convex domain Ω_1 can be expressed as an intersection of closed half spaces:

$$\bar{\Omega}_1 = \bigcap_{\mu\in R^2} \{\boldsymbol{\beta} \in \boldsymbol{R}^2; \boldsymbol{\mu} \cdot \boldsymbol{\beta} \leq C_\mu\}.$$

Now, for each $\mu \in \mathbf{R}^2$, $\mu \cdot \alpha \in C(\bar{\Omega})$ is harmonic, and by the weak maximum principle we have

$$\mu \cdot \alpha(x) \leq C_\mu, \quad \forall x \in \bar{\Omega}.$$

Thus $\alpha(\Omega) \subseteq \Omega_1$. However, since an $(n-1)$-*sphere* cannot be a retract of an $n - ball$ (by a corollary to Brouwer's theorem [23]), we should have $\alpha(\Omega) = \Omega_1$. □

Let us now state a key result that seems to require a strong hypothesis on the smoothness of the boundary data.

LEMMA 10.3.4. *Let α be the optimal solution corresponding to the prescribed boundary homeomorphism $g \in H^{3/2+\epsilon}(\partial\Omega)$ of $\partial\Omega$ onto the boundary $\partial\Omega_1$ of a convex set Ω_1. Then*

$$J_\alpha(x) = \mathrm{Det}\nabla\alpha \neq 0, \quad \forall x \in \Omega.$$

Proof of this result involves complex variable methods and can be found in [63].

The following result is a special case of a result in [63]. We should observe that in this particular lemma, Ω_1 *need not be convex and also α need not be a harmonic map.*

LEMMA 10.3.5. *Let Ω and Ω_1 be homeomorphic images of the unit disk. Suppose $\alpha : \bar{\Omega} \to \bar{\Omega}_1$ is a differentiable surjective transformation such that:*

(i) $\alpha : \partial\Omega \to \partial\Omega_1$ *is a homeomorphism onto map, and*

(ii) $J_\alpha(x) \neq 0$, *for all $x \in \Omega$.*

Then $\alpha(\Omega) = \Omega_1$, and α is a homeomorphism from $\bar{\Omega}$ onto $\bar{\Omega}_1$.

Proof. We will prove this result using the same method as in [63] but with a different definition for the degree of the map α. This will allow us to discuss the possibility of removing the differentiability hypothesis on α.

For any $y = \alpha(x)$ with $y \notin \partial\Omega$, the degree of the map α is defined as in [59]:

(10.15)
$$\mathcal{D}_\alpha(y; \Omega) = \int_\Omega f_\epsilon(\alpha(x))J_\alpha(x)dx,$$

where $f_\epsilon(\cdot) : \mathbf{R}^2 \to \mathbf{R}$ is a family of continuous transformations such that

$$\int_{\Omega_1} f_\epsilon(x)dx = 1,$$

and Supp $f_\epsilon = B(y; \epsilon)$ is the ball of sufficiently small radius ϵ centered at y.

If the sign of $J_\alpha(x)$ is constant (i.e., if $J_\alpha(x) \neq 0$, for all $x \in \Omega$), then $\mathcal{D}_\alpha(y; \Omega) = \pm$ Number of solutions x for a given y with $y = \alpha(x)$. This means that the degree of the map α in this case is equal to the number of points in Ω that are mapped to the point $y \in \Omega_1$ under the map α. Note that in (10.15), in order for the integral to make sense, we need only $J_\alpha(\cdot) \in L^1(\Omega)$. This will be the case when $\alpha \in H^1(\Omega)$, since $\nabla\alpha \in L^2(\Omega)$ implies that Det $\nabla\alpha \in L^1(\Omega)$.

Let us now provide arguments to show that the degree of α is ± 1.

Let us recall the following general result for regular maps given in [23].

PROPOSITION 10.3.1. *Let* $\boldsymbol{\alpha}$ *be a continuous map such that*

$$\boldsymbol{\alpha} : (B^n, \partial B^n) \to (B^n, \partial B^n),$$

where B^n *is the n-ball and* ∂B^n *denotes the* $(n-1)$*-sphere. Let* $\boldsymbol{\alpha}_b$ *be the restriction of* $\boldsymbol{\alpha}$ *to* ∂B^n :

$$\boldsymbol{\alpha}_b = \boldsymbol{\alpha}|_{\partial B^n} : \partial B^n \to \partial B^n.$$

Then

$$Degree \ of \ \boldsymbol{\alpha}_b = \ Degree \ of \ \boldsymbol{\alpha}.$$

Moreover, if $\boldsymbol{\alpha}_b : \partial B^n \to \partial B^n$ *is a homeomorphism, then*

$$Degree \ of \ \boldsymbol{\alpha}_b = \pm 1.$$

This is precisely the situation we have, and hence

$$\pm 1 = \int_\Omega f_\epsilon(\boldsymbol{\alpha}(\boldsymbol{x})) J_\alpha(\boldsymbol{x}) d\boldsymbol{x}.$$

But $J_\alpha(\boldsymbol{x}) \neq 0$, for all $\boldsymbol{x} \in \Omega$ (nonzero almost everywhere in Ω if $J_\alpha(\cdot) \in L^1(\Omega)$). Therefore, for each $\boldsymbol{y} \in \Omega_1$, there exists exactly one $\boldsymbol{x} \in \Omega$ such that $\boldsymbol{\alpha}(\boldsymbol{x}) = \boldsymbol{y}$. Thus $\boldsymbol{\alpha}$ is bijective on Ω and by standard results [23], $\boldsymbol{\alpha}$ is a homeomorphism.   □

10.4. Harmonic Grids in Three Dimensions

It appears that only a part of the theory developed in §10.3 (Lemmas 10.3.3 and 10.3.5) extends immediately to the three-dimensional case. Let us indicate in this section the available results for three dimensions and outline a key open problem.

LEMMA 10.4.1. *Let* $\Omega \subset \boldsymbol{R}^3$ *be a bounded open set with* $\partial\Omega$ *of class* C^2 *and let* $\Omega_1 \subset \boldsymbol{R}^3$ *be a convex bounded domain. Suppose that the optimal solution* $\boldsymbol{\alpha}$ *can be obtained by specifying the boundary homeomorphism* $\boldsymbol{\alpha} : \partial\Omega \to \partial\Omega_1$:

$$\boldsymbol{\alpha}|_{\partial\Omega} = \boldsymbol{g} \in H^{1+\epsilon}(\partial\Omega).$$

Then $\boldsymbol{\alpha}$ *maps* $\bar\Omega$ *onto* $\bar\Omega_1$.

The proof is the same as that for Lemma 10.3.5. We need only to note that $\boldsymbol{\alpha} \in H^{3/2+\epsilon}(\Omega) \subset C(\bar\Omega)$ for the three-dimensional case.

LEMMA 10.4.2. *Let* Ω *and* Ω_1 *be homeomorphic images of the unit ball. Suppose* $\boldsymbol{\alpha} : \bar\Omega \to \bar\Omega_1$ *to be a differentiable surjective transformation such that*

(i) $\boldsymbol{\alpha} : \partial\Omega \to \partial\Omega_1$ *is a homeomorphism onto map, and*

(ii) $J_\alpha(\boldsymbol{x}) \neq 0$, *for all* $\boldsymbol{x} \in \Omega$.

Then $\boldsymbol{\alpha}(\Omega) = \Omega_1$, *and* $\boldsymbol{\alpha}$ *is a homeomorphism from* $\bar\Omega$ *onto* $\bar\Omega_1$.

The proof is again the same as that for Lemma 10.3.5. Note that in order for the degree integral to make sense, we need $J_\alpha(\cdot) \in L^1(\Omega)$, and this will in turn require that $\nabla\alpha \in L^3(\Omega)$.

Also note that in order to show that the harmonic map is a grid-generating transform in three dimensions, we need a result of the type given in Lemma 10.3.4 which is not available.

OPEN PROBLEM 10.1. *Let $\Omega \subset \boldsymbol{R}^3$ be a bounded open set with $\partial\Omega$ of class C^2, and let $\Omega_1 \subset \boldsymbol{R}^3$ be a convex bounded domain. Suppose that $\boldsymbol{\alpha}$ is the optimal solution corresponding to the prescribed boundary homeomorphism $\boldsymbol{g} \in H^{2+\epsilon}(\partial\Omega)$ of $\partial\Omega$ onto $\partial\Omega_1$. Show that*

$$J_\alpha(\boldsymbol{x}) = \mathrm{Det}\nabla\boldsymbol{\alpha} \neq 0, \qquad \forall \boldsymbol{x} \in \Omega.$$

References

[1] W.F. AMES, *Numerical Methods for Partial Differential Equations*, Second Edition, Academic Press, New York, 1977, p. 83.

[2] A.A. AMSDEN AND C.W. HIRT, *A simple scheme for generating general curvilinear grids*, J. Comput. Phys., 11 (1973), pp. 348–359.

[3] D.A. ANDERSON, *Adaptive grid scheme controlling cell area/volume*, AIAA-87-0202, AIAA 25th Aerospace Sciences Meeting, Reno, NV, January 12–15, 1987.

[4] ———, *Equidistributive Schemes, Poisson Generator, and Adaptive Grids*, Elsevier, Amsterdam, 1987; Appl. Math. Comput., 24(1987), pp. 211–227.

[5] V. BARBU AND TH. PRECUPANU, *Convexity and Optimization in Banach Spaces*, Riedel, Boston, 1985.

[6] W.D. BARFIELD, *An optimal mesh generator for Lagrangian hydrodynamic calculations in two space dimensions*, J. Comput. Phys., 6(1970), pp. 417–429.

[7] P. BARRERA-SANCHEZ AND J.E. CASTILLO, *A large scale optimization problem arising from numerical grid generation*, Tech. Report, Department of Mathematics and Statistics, University of New Mexico, Albuquerque, NM, 1987.

[8] J. BIGGE AND E. BOHL, *Deformations of the bifurcation diagram due to discretization*, Math. Comp., 45(1985), pp. 393–403.

[9] G. BIRKHOFF AND R.E. LYNCH, *Numerical solution of elliptic problems*, SIAM Studies in Applied Mathematics, Society for Industrial and Applied Mathematics, Philadelphia, PA 1984.

[10] J.P. BOURGUINON AND H. BREZIS, *Remarks on the Euler equations*, J. Funct. Anal., 15(1974), pp. 341–363.

[11] J.U. BRACKBILL AND J.S. SALTZMAN, *Adaptive zoning for singular problems in two dimensions*, J. Comput. Phys., 46(1982), pp. 342–368.

[12] J.U. BRACKBILL, *Coordinate system control: Adaptive meshes*, in Numerical Grid Generation, J.F. Thompson, ed., North–Holland, Amsterdam, 1982, pp. 277–288.

[13] J.E. CASTILLO, *A direct variational grid generation method*, in Advances in Computer Methods for Partial Differential Equations VI, International Association for Mathematics and Computers in Simulation, New Brunswick, NJ, 1987, pp. 501–506.

[14] ———, *A direct variational grid generation method: Orthogonality control*, in Numerical Grid Generation in Computational Fluid Mechanics '88, S. Sengupta, J. Häuser, P.R. Eiseman, and J.F. Thompson, eds., Pineridge Press Limited,

Swansea, U.K., 1988, pp. 247–256.

[15] ——, *A discrete variational grid generation method*, SIAM J. Sci. Statist. Comput., 12 (1991), pp. 454–468.

[16] ——, *Mathematical aspects of variational grid generation* I, in Numerical Grid Generation in Fluid Dynamics, J. Häuser and C. Taylor, eds., Pineridge Press Limited, Swansea, U.K., 1986, pp. 35–44.

[17] J.E. CASTILLO, S. STEINBERG, AND P.J. ROACHE, *Mathematical aspects of variational grid generation* II, J. Comp. Appl. Math., 20(1987), pp. 127–135.

[18] ——, *On the folding of numerical grids: Use of reference grids*, Comm. Appl. Numer. Methods , 4(1988), pp. 471–481.

[19] J.E. CASTILLO, *On variational grid generation*, Ph.D. thesis, Department of Mathematics, University of New Mexico, Albuquerque, NM, 1987.

[20] J.E. CASTILLO, S. STEINBERG, AND P.J. ROACHE, *Parameter estimation in variational grid generation*, Appl. Math. Comput., 28(1988), pp. 155–177.

[21] W.H. CHU, *Development of a general finite difference approximation for a general domain; Part* I: *Machine transformation*, J. Comput. Phys., 8(1971), pp. 392–408.

[22] C. DALTON, CHAIR, *First National Fluid Dynamics Congress*, AIAA/ASME/SIAM/APS, Cincinnati, OH, July 1988.

[23] J. DUGUNDJI, *Topology*, Allyn and Bacon, Boston, 1966.

[24] A.S. DVINSKY, *Adaptive grid generation from harmonic maps*, in Numerical Grid Generation in Computational Fluid Mechanics '88, S. Sengupta, J. Häuser, P.R. Eiseman, and J.F. Thompson, eds., Pineridge Press Limited, Swansea, U.K., 1988.

[25] ——, *Adaptive grid generation from harmonic maps on Riemannian manifolds*, NSF Report TM-1316, Creare Inc., Hanover, NH, 1987.

[26] ——, *Adaptive grid generation from harmonic maps on Riemannian manifolds*, J. Comput. Phys., submitted.

[27] J. EELLS AND L. LEMAIRE, *A report on harmonic maps*, Bull. London Math. Soc., 10(1978), pp. 1–68.

[28] J. EELLS AND J.H. SAMPSON, *Harmonic mappings of Riemannian manifolds*, American J. Math., 86(1964), pp. 109–160.

[29] P.R. EISEMAN, *Grid generation for fluid mechanics computations*, Ann. Rev. Fluid Mech., 17(1985), pp. 487–522.

[30] R. FLETCHER, *Unconstrained Optimization*, John Wiley and Sons, New York, 1980.

[31] F.B. FULLER, *Harmonic Mappings*, Proc. Nat. Acad. Sci., 40(1954), p. 987–991.

[32] K.N. GHIA AND U. GHIA, EDS., *Advances in grid generation*, in Proc. Applied Mechanics, Bioengineering, and Fluids Engineering Conference, Houston, TX, June 1983.

[33] U. GHIA, CHAIR, AIAA 8*th Computational Fluid Dynamics Conference*, Cincinnati, OH, 1985.

[34] B. GILDING, *A numerical grid generation technique*, Comput. & Fluids, 16(1988), pp. 47–58.

[35] S.K. GODUNOV AND G.P. PROKOPOV, *The use of moving meshes in gas-dynamical computations*, USSR Comput. Math. and Math. Phys., 12(1972), pp. 182–195.

[36] R. HAMILTON, *Harmonic maps of manifolds with boundary*, Lecture Notes in Computer Science 471, Springer-Verlag, Berlin, Heidelberg, New York, 1975.

[37] J. HÄUSER AND C. TAYLOR, EDS., *Proc. Numerical Grid Generation in Fluid*

Dynamics Conference, Landshut, W. Germany, 1986.

[38] S. HILDEBRANDT, *Harmonic mapping of Riemannian manifolds*, Lecture Notes in Mathematics 1161, Springer-Verlag, Berlin, New York, 1985.

[39] F. JOHN, *Partial Differential Equations*, Springer-Verlag, New York, 1986.

[40] J. JOST, *Harmonic maps between surfaces*, Lecture Notes in Mathematics 1062, Springer-Verlag, Berlin, New York, 1985.

[41] ———, *Lectures on harmonic maps (with applications to conformal mappings and minimal surfaces)*, Lecture Notes in Mathematics 1161, Springer-Verlag, Berlin, New York, 1985.

[42] S.R. KENNON AND G.S. DULIKRAVICH, *A posteriori optimization of computational grids*, AIAA paper N_0, 85-0483, presented at the AIAA 23rd Aerospace Science Meeting, Reno, NV, January 1985.

[43] P.M. KNUPP, *Surface grid generation in the tangent plane*, Numer. Methods Partial Differential Equations, to appear.

[44] E. KREYSZIG, *Differential Geometry*, University of Toronto Press, Toronto, Ontario, Canada, 1959.

[45] H. LEWY, *On the minimum number of domains in which the nodal lines of spherical harmonics divide the sphere*, Comm. Partial Differential Equations, 2(1977), pp. 1233–1244.

[46] G. LIAO, *A regularity theorem for harmonic maps with small energy*, J. Differential Geom., 22(1985), pp. 233–241.

[47] V.D. LISEIKIN AND N.N. YANENKO, *On selection of optimal finite-difference grids*, Numer. Meth. Continuum Mech., 8(1977), pp. 100–104. (In Russian.)

[48] C.W. MASTIN AND J.F. THOMPSON, *Elliptic systems and numerical transformations*, J. Math. Anal. Appl., 62(1978), pp. 52–62.

[49] ———, *Quasiconformal mappings and grid generation*, SIAM J. Sci. Statist. Comput., 5(1984), pp. 305–310.

[50] ———, *Transformation of three-dimensional regions onto rectangular regions by elliptic systems*, Numer. Math., 29(1978), pp. 397–407.

[51] C.W. MISNER, *Harmonic maps as models for physical theories*, Phys. Rev. D, 18(1978), pp. 4510–4524.

[52] L. NIRENBERG, private communication, 1986.

[53] H.O. PEITGEN, D. SAUPE, AND K. SCHMITT, *Nonlinear elliptic boundary value problems versus their finite difference approximations: Numerically irrelevant solutions*, J. Reine Angew. Math., 322(1981), pp. 74–117.

[54] M.H. PROTTER AND H.F. WEINBERGER, *Maximum Principles in Differential Equations*, Prentice–Hall, Englewood Cliffs, NJ, 1967.

[55] T. RADO, *Aufgabe 41*, Jahresbericht der Deutschen Mathematiker Vereinigung, 35(1926), p. 49.

[56] J. SACKS AND K. UHLENBECK, *The existence of minimal immersions of 2-spheres*, Ann. of Math., 113(1981), pp. 1–24.

[57] R. SCHOEN AND S.-T. YAU, *On univalent harmonic maps between surfaces*, Invent. Math., 44(1978), pp. 265–278.

[58] R. SCHOEN AND K. UHLENBECK, *Boundary regularity and the Dirichlet problem for harmonic maps*, J. Differential Geom., 18 (1983), pp. 253–268.

[59] J.T. SCHWARTZ, *Nonlinear Functional Analysis*, Gordon and Breach, New York, 1969.

[60] S. SENGUPTA, J. HÄUSER, P.R. EISEMAN, AND J.F. THOMPSON, EDS., *Numerical Grid Generation in Computational Fluid Mechanics '88*, Pineridge Press Limited, Swansea, U.K., 1988.

[61] D.F. SHANNO, *Conjugate gradient methods with inexact searches*, Math. Oper. Res., 3(1978), pp. 244–256.

[62] R.E. SHOWALTER, *Hilbert Space Methods For Partial Differential Equations*, Pitman, London, 1977.

[63] P.W. SMITH AND S.S. SRITHARAN, *Theory of harmonic grid generation*, Complex Variables, 10(1988), pp. 359–369.

[64] S.S. SRITHARAN, *Invariant Manifold Theory For Hydrodynamic Transition*, Longman, London, 1990.

[65] S. STEINBERG AND P.J. ROACHE, *Anomalies in grid generation on curves*, J. Comput. Phys., to appear.

[66] ——, *Variational curve and surface grid generation*, J. Comput. Phys., submitted.

[67] ——, *Variational grid generation*, Numer. Methods Partial Differential Equations, 2(1986), pp. 71–96.

[68] D.J. STRUIK, *Lectures on Classical Differential Geometry*, Addison–Wesley, Reading, MA, 1950.

[69] A. STUART, *Nonlinear instability in dissipative finite difference schemes*, SIAM Rev., 31(1989), pp. 191–220.

[70] R. TEMAM, *Navier–Stokes Equations*, Third Edition, North–Holland, Amsterdam, 1984.

[71] J.F. THOMPSON, *A survey of dynamically-adaptive grids in the numerical solution of partial differential equations*, Appl. Numer. Math., 1(1985), pp. 3–27.

[72] ——, *Grid generation techniques in computational fluid dynamics*, AIAA J., 22(1984), pp. 1505–1523.

[73] J.F. THOMPSON, ED., *Numerical Grid Generation*, Elsevier, Amsterdam, 1982.

[74] J.F. THOMPSON, F.C. THAMES, AND C.E. MASTIN, *Automatic numerical generation of body-fitted curvilinear coordinate systems for a field containing any number of arbitrary two-dimensional bodies*, J. Comput. Phys., 15(1974), pp. 299–319.

[75] J.F. THOMPSON, Z.U.A. WARSI, AND C.W. MASTIN, *Numerical Grid Generation: Foundations and Applications*, North–Holland, Amsterdam, 1985.

[76] ——, *Boundary-fitted coordinate systems for numerical solutions of partial differential equations—a review*, J. Comput. Phys., 47(1982), pp. 1–109.

[77] W.N. TIARN, Ph.D. thesis, Department of Aerospace Engineering, Mississippi State University, Mississippi State, MS, May 1988.

[78] VAX UNIX MACSYMA *Reference Manual*, Version 11, Symbolics, Inc., Cambridge, MA, 1985.

[79] Z.U.A. WARSI, *A note on the mathematical formulation of the problem of numerical coordinate generation*, Quart. Appl. Math., 41 (1983), pp. 221–236.

[80] ——, *A synopsis of elliptic PDE models for grid generation*, Appl. Math. Comput., 21(1987), pp. 295–311.

[81] ——, *Basic differential models for coordinate generation*, in Numerical Grid Generation, J.F. Thompson, ed., North–Holland, Amsterdam, 1982, pp. 41–70.

[82] ——, *Numerical grid generation in arbitrary surfaces through a second-order differential-geometric model*, J. Comput. Phys., 64(1986), pp. 82-96.

[83] ——, *Theoretical foundation of the equations for the generation of surface coordinates*, AIAA J., to appear.

[84] T.J. WILLMORE, *An Introduction to Differential Geometry*, Oxford University Press, Oxford, U.K., 1959.

[85] A.M. WINSLOW, *Numerical solution of the quasilinear Poisson equation in a*

nonuniform triangle mesh, J. Comput. Phys., 2(1967), pp. 149–172.

[86] N.N. YANENKO, N.T. DANAEV, AND V.D. LISEIKIN, *On a variational method for grid generation*, Numer. Meth. Continuum Mech., 7(1977), pp. 157–163. (In Russian.)

[87] P.R. EISEMAN, *A multi-surface method of coordinate generation*, J. Comput. Phys., 33(1979), pp. 118–150.

Index